Mobilizing Democracy

Changing the U.S. Role
in the Middle East

Edited by Greg Bates

Common Courage Press   Monroe, Maine

Randy Kehler's "Towards a Pro-Democracy Move-
ment in the United States" originally appeared in *The
Nation* magazine/The Nation, Inc. © 1990, under the title
"Anti-War Means Pro-Democracy; The Peace Movement
Now—II" and is reprinted by permission.

Manning Marable's "The Quest for Empire and the
Struggle for Peace and Justice" is taken from his column
"Along the Color Line" which appears in over 170 news-
papers internationally.

Cynthia Enloe's "Womenandchildren" originally appeared in the *Village Voice*.

Howard Zinn's "Failure to Quit: Why Activism is
Worth It" is a revised and updated article which originally
appeared in *Z Magazine*.

Library of Congress Cataloging-in-Publication Data
Because of federal budget cutbacks, CIP data is
temporarily unavailable for books from new publishers.

ISBN: 0-9628838-0-8 paper,   0-9628838-1-6 cloth

Common Courage Press
P.O. Box 702
Corner of Jackson Rd & Rte 139
Monroe, ME 04951
207-525-0900

Table of Contents

Acknowledgements   v

I. The Road To War

An Interview with Noam Chomsky and Eqbal Ahmad
by Rabab Hadi
The Gulf Crisis: How We Got Here   3

An Interview with Abbas Nasrawi and Naseer Aruri
by Rabab Hadi
"From We Pay, You Fight to You Pay, We Fight"   25

Jeanne Butterfield
Taking a Stand Against the Double Standard   35

Sheila Ryan
Power Projection in the Middle East:
Maintaining Control at Any Cost   41

Cyrus Bina
War Over Access to Cheap Oil,
or the Reassertion of U.S. Hegemony?
Debunking a Popular Myth   71

Manning Marable
The Quest For Empire
and the Struggle For Peace and Justice   83

Cynthia Enloe
"WomenandChildren:"
Propaganda Tools of Patriarchy   89

II. Seizing Opportunities for Change

Howard Zinn
Failure to Quit: Is Activism Worth It?   99

Stephen Zunes
The Gulf Crisis and Opportunities
for Social Change   107

Denis F. Doyon
Creating an "Iraq Syndrome"   125

III. Short- and Long-Term Tasks for Peace

Michael Marsh
Encouraging Dissent From Within:
Working with Conscientious Objectors   137

Erik Larsen
Refusal to Participate in Interventionist Wars   147

Sam Lwin
The Fox Company, not the Box Company   151

Nancy Murray and Hady Amr
Reclaiming Democracy: Congress and the Creation
of a Just Middle East Policy   163

Randy Kehler
Towards a Pro-Democracy Movement
in the United States   181

Robert A. Irwin
Beyond Crisis Response:
Building a Peace System   191

Appendix: Organizations   211

About the Contributors   215

About Common Courage Press   218

Acknowledgements

One of the lessons in taking on a Herculean task—such as getting this book together with tight time and money constraints—is realizing how many people there are who rush to shoulder the burden once you have begun.

The authors in this book are, without exception, activists. Their patience with my insistence that they must contribute despite already overburdened schedules as each fought to stop the impending war was extraordinary. They understood that a commitment to act is strengthened by convincing others to do likewise. Thus this volume. As an indication of their commitment, many authors have donated their share of the royalties to support material aid projects for Palestinians in the West Bank and Gaza. A remarkable statement of the developing consensus that the resolution of the question of Palestine must be part of a just end to this crisis.

South End Press and New Society Publishers were generous with their material support. South End offered free use of a laser printer. New Society assisted in marketing the book.

Laura Reiner went beyond the call of duty, volunteering to do editing and proofreading, without which this book would not have been readable. Her willingness to help at a moment's notice kept this book on schedule.

Andrea Stark also helped with production, and provided invaluable assistance finding local help to accomplish several tasks.

Marie Bloom gave much needed encouragement in the early days of the project—at a time when creating this book seemed an impossible task.

Chris Cartter of Grassroots International suggested a number of contributors to this volume, including Nancy Murray of the Middle East Justice Network, and Eqbal

Ahmad.

Robert Irwin's editorial advice and willingness to help solve a number of problems posed by the nature of publishing an anthology was a solid contribution.

This book would not have seen the light of day without Flic Shooter. Her ability to listen to problems and provide brilliant solutions, diligent work, and commitment to being organized improved the book immensely. Her editorial creativity was a major contribution to the book's coherence.

Support from people in our local community helped the book through a number of bottlenecks: Ed McCurdy and Susan McCurdy provided a computer and transportation at several key points; Lauren Murray supplied enthusiasm at just the right time to help me push on.

Finally, with the consolidation of the publishing industry and the pernicious obedience of the media to government propaganda, it is to friends that I have turned for help in getting this book into people's hands.

Part I
The Road to War

The Gulf Crisis
How We Got Here

Interview with Noam Chomsky and Eqbal Ahmad by Rabab Hadi

November 17, 1990

The Senate and House debates leading up to the beginning of war with Iraq on January 16 were largely over tactics: should sanctions against Iraq be given more time to work, or should Congress support the president to use force immediately if necessary to remove Iraqi forces from Kuwait? Hidden from the discussion was any mention of U.S. interests in the region, either in the current crisis or historically. In this interview, Noam Chomsky and Eqbal Ahmad offer perspectives on the political forces guiding U.S. policy in the Middle East. It is not the principle that aggression must not be rewarded which has led the United States to war, they argue. Rather, there are other motivations, including the control of oil and the defeat of nationalist movements in the third world, which determine U.S. actions.

Hadi: How would you characterize the current U.S. policy in the Middle East? Does it represent a new direction or a continuation of past policy? What are the points *vis a vis* the Gulf crisis and the Palestine question?

Chomsky: There is a traditional policy and it undergoes various tactical alterations as conditions change, but the basic thrust of policy remains the same and it has

3

been the same for a long time. By the 1940s, it was well understood that the world's major cheap and abundant energy resources are in the Arabian Peninsula and the Gulf region. It was also understood that whoever has a dominant role in controlling those resources is in a very strong position to dominate the world. The United States perceived itself in the 1940s as a dominant world power—the world's first global power able to run the world. To do that, it wanted to make sure that it controlled the energy resources, which it regarded as crucial for world domination.

Prior to the 1940s, the French, the British and the Americans had divided up the resources of the region on the 1920 Red Line agreement. The first move that was made after the Second World War was to kick out the French. They were excluded under the pretext that they were an enemy country because they had been occupied by the Germans and therefore their role in the Red Line agreement was abrogated. So that left it to the British and Americans. The American role in control of the Middle East oil continually increased through that period while the British role declined. But that was just a reflection of their general power relations. The United States wanted to keep Britain viable because it is considered a loyal client state. So, therefore, it does want Britain in Kuwait and the United States was happy to let the British control the oil and investments from Kuwait while the United States took the big prizes for itself like Saudi Arabia, where it has been dominant.

One corollary to this is that no indigenous force is permitted to gain significant influence or control over Middle East oil. In fact, that is a more general policy applied beyond the Middle East. The United States is opposed to independent nationalism anywhere in the third world. That is official policy for an obvious reason: indigenous nationalism means that people will try to use resources for their own purposes and carry out their own economic development. But the third world is there to be exploited by the industrial powers, not to serve its own interests. So in the Middle East, the consequence of this principle is that no indigenous force is permitted to get extensive control over Middle East oil. That has to be controlled by the United States, by U.S. energy corporations, by loyal client states like Britain, or by loyal domestic clients like the Saudi Arabian elites or the Gulf Emirates or the Kuwaiti elites. Any arrangement is acceptable, as long as they basically act the way the United States tells them to. They are allowed to play their role. They are regarded as Harvard Business School graduates who happen to wear *kaffiahs*, but other than that, we don't care about them so much.

On the other hand, if any indigenous nationalist movement develops, the United States is opposed. That is official policy. The first explicit trace I can find is in 1958, when the National Security Council memorandum determined that a logical corollary of their opposition to radical Arab nationalism—that means independent Arab nationalism—is support for Israel as the only reliable pro-U.S. regime in the region. At that time, they were worried about Nasser. Prior to that, they were worried about Mossadeq. Later, they worried about Khomeini. And now they are worried about Saddam Hussein. But it could be anybody who could be anywhere in the political spectrum. Mossadeq, Nasser, Khomeini, and Hussein have nothing in common with each other, except that they were all radical nationalists. They were all moving towards the direction where the Arab world, the Islamic world or the Middle East might get control of its own resources. That is unacceptable and we can see another version of that today.

Hadi: Eqbal, how would you address the difference, if any, in U.S. policy in the Middle East in the stage before 1979, during the fall of the Shah, and after that period?

Ahmad: I would begin by reinforcing what Noam has been saying. There is more continuity than there is change in American objectives in the Middle East. That is why, since the end of World War II, the region has produced more Hitlers in American demonology than any other region. Mossadeq was portrayed as a Hitler, then Abdul Nasser as Hitler. His book, *Philosophy of the Revolution,* was described by the *New York Times* and the *Washington Post* as the equivalent of *Mein Kampf.* Then Arafat was portrayed as Hitler. Most people do not recall that until 1977, and even in '78, Anwar Sadat was portrayed as a Hitler, including in several articles in the *New York Times.* Then Khomeini was portrayed as a Hitler and now Saddam Hussein is a Hitler. Hitler and Munich are, in the postwar period, in the centrality of the American interest. In that sense, there is much more continuity than there is change.

I would, however, emphasize that there has been significant change which has intensified American hegemony as a world power. By 1968, most of the other pillars of American predominance in the world had either fallen or weakened. Its strategic superiority, by which I mean superiority in the production and delivery of nuclear weapons, was challenged by the attainment of nuclear parity by the Soviet Union. Its economic predominance was undermined by the achievement of equality by powers which previously had been junior partners of the United States, namely Europe and Japan. Its capacity to police the world had been challenged by the experience of Vietnam, which rendered the invisible wars visible, forgotten wars remembered, and limited wars unlimited in their consequences for the United States. In that situation, if you really remain committed to the notion of staying the number 1 power in the world, you will lean on the last pillar you have left. And for the United States that is the pillar of controlling the resources of the world, without which the industrialized world cannot be, cannot survive, cannot exist fully. And also, without which the third world cannot really survive.

Chomsky: Eqbal is exactly correct. The more far-sighted of the U.S. planners already perceived back in the 1940s that these problems would arise. Among them was George Kennan, one of the major architects of U.S. policy after the Second World War and the chairman of the State Department's Policy Planning Staff. He was particularly involved in the reconstruction of Germany and Japan, which was a major U.S. policy after the war. Regarding Japan particularly, he said in 1949 that the United States should permit Japan to reindustrialize and in fact encourage it to do so within the American system with one limitation. The United States should control its energy and in that way, he said, we can insure what he called the "veto power" of whatever Japan may do some day. And that was very farsighted, because at that time, nobody thought that Japan would be a competitor. In fact, until the mid-1960s they were trying to keep the Japanese economy viable. But Kennan forsaw the contingency that Eqbal was describing, and that at some point down the road we would have to exercise that "veto power." Meaning we have to have a stranglehold on Europe and Japan.

Ahmad: And they tried to exercise it. In fact, we should remind ourselves that, to the credit of the Middle Eastern people, there was more than one American effort to implement this design. Two years after the founding of NATO, the U.S. policymakers had designed a detailed plan for METO, the Middle East Treaty Organization, which was also known at one time as MEDO, the Middle East Defense Organization. By 1953-54, the United States had started entering into bilateral mutual defense agreements with key Middle Eastern countries: Pakistan, Turkey, Iran, Jordan and Iraq. Iraq under King Faisal and Nouri Said. By 1956-57, the Baghdad Pact was fully at work. During this entire period of what began as the Truman doctrine, grew into the Eisenhower doctrine, and on through to the Nixon and Carter doctrines, nearly every American president had a design on the Middle East that was frustrated by Middle Eastern nationalism. It was either Mossadeq or Nasser or a group of Algerians, Syrians, and Ba'athist Iraqis and others coalescing. The force of Arab nationalism—the anti-imperialist component of Middle Eastern nationalism, I should say—has frustrated Amerian designs consistantly.

What is unique about the present period is that U.S. designs have intensified for reasons we just recalled. As well, the Arab national movement has never been as weak since the 1900s as it is today. Fragmentation of the Arab and Middle Eastern countries by the consolidation of the state system has been to the advantage of the United States. And this is why policymakers feel angry about somebody like Saddam Hussein. He broke that law by calling for Arab unity. And that is intolerable.

Hadi: You both talked about the period following the Second World War. I'd like you to address the question of U.S. foreign policy after the end of the Cold War. How is the Gulf crisis different from conflicts before the end of the Cold War and the change in Soviet-U.S. relations?

Chomsky: I think that the departure of the Soviet Union from the world scene had several effects on U.S. policy and that of Germany and Japan. Traditionally, Russia was a quasi-colonial backyard that provided Western Europe with resources and cheap labor and so on. And that is exactly what they want to return it to. In fact, a large part of the Cold War is exactly about that. The Russians were like these independent nationalists in that they closed off a part of the world from Western exploitation. And that, like Arab nationalism, is also intolerable. National Security Council Memo 68 (NSC 68), which

Eqbal quoted before, said in the 1950s that our goal is to break up the Soviet Union into successive states, which means to return it to its traditional pre-1917 role. And that is one thing that has changed. Now there is a new third world opening up, including oil resources in Siberia, which Japan may soon be trying to exploit for itself.

Secondly, until its departure, the Soviet Union was a deterrent. Western propaganda talked about deterrence and containment as if we were deterring and containing the Russians. In fact it was the other way around—they were deterring and containing the United States. The United States is a global power. The Russians could be as violent as they liked, but in their own region. They were not a global power. But Soviet power did contain and deter the United States. There was always the concern in the case of intervention in the third world that if the United States went too far, it might enter into a confrontation with the Russians. And that is dangerous because they are powerful. That was particularly true in the Middle East. In every intervention in the Middle East there has been a concern over a confrontation with the Russians. It was true in '58 and in '67. In fact, then-Secretary of Defense McNamara said that "we damn near had war" in 1967, when there was an actual confrontation between the Russian and American fleets in the eastern Mediterranean. Then in 1973, there was a nuclear alert, and so on. Every single time there was always that threat. That put a limit on U.S. actions. Certainly in Vietnam, the United States was always worried about going too far, because that might get the Russians involved and that would harm us.

Another change is that the Russians provided some kind of aid and support to targets of U.S. intervention and that is another kind of deterrence: it makes it harder to intervene. The United States is now free to do what it likes. It can send forces to the Gulf, without any concern for the consequences. While the Russians were still around, it could not have done that. It wasn't the fear that the Russians would intervene. Rather, it was the fear that a major military action near the Russian borders might just blow up into a superpower confrontation. Military actions are uncontrollable once they start; what happens next isn't predictable. But now the fear of confrontation with the Soviets is gone, so there is no deterrent to U.S. force. It is the dominant world power from a military point of view (though not from an economic point of view). This change is a major consequence of Soviet withdrawal from the world scene. It means we can expect more violence.

Ahmad: I would totally agree. I've nothing to add except a few footnotes to what Noam has said. In 1956, the United States would not have leaned on its allies to withdraw from Egypt if it had not been for the Russian ultimatum. In 1982, the Israelis probably would have run through the Bekaa Valley and possibly right up to Damascus if it were not for the fear of a Russian response. In 1973, had the Russians not aided the Egyptians, the crossing of the Suez Canal would have been impossible. When the Israelis had turned it around following the nuclear alert, the Israelis might have gone on to destroy Cairo, were it not for the Soviet deterrent. So the Soviet Union was a limiting factor; that limit on the exercise of American power has been reduced.

The second statement Noam made is also one to which I would like to add a major footnote. He spoke of the desire by the United States to see the Soviets broken up into smaller countries and exploited. This effort at dismemberment was probably most dramatically demonstrated in U.S. policies in Afghanistan following 1985. The Soviets intervened in Afghanistan in 1981. During this period, the United States supplied escalating amounts of money and armament through Pakistan to the Mujahadeen. In 1983 the money supplied totalled roughly $100 million. By 1986 it amounted to $680 million and then $710 million in 1987. Before that, in 1985, the Russians had clearly indicated that they wanted to withdraw from Afghanistan. The Americans did not want that withdrawal. They upped the ante and the Russians, by 1987-88, agreed to accept all American conditions and all Pakistani conditions for withdrawal. Even then they upped the ante. Finally the Russians withdrew, and they withdrew according to the timetable given to them by the United Nations.

But the United States did not honor the agreement made through the U.N., namely that during the Russian withdrawal the United States would stop their support to the Mujahadeen. Support to the Mujahadeen has continued in violation of the UN accord even today. Why this support after withdrawal? The reasons were the following: Afghanistan is one country among others which has a long border with the Soviet Union and a long border with Iran. What the Americans are looking for is an opportunity, when the moment arrives, to be able to intervene in Iran, to bring about a regime favorable to U.S. interests. In addition, if the United States were to gain bases in Afghanistan some day, it would be able to intervene in central Asian republics with which Afghanistan has not only borders but tribal contiguity. This contiguity—where the same people speak the same language on both sides of the border—makes covert operations possible. I have written some on it and there is a lot of documentation available if you are willing to look for it.

This policy of support in Afghanistan provides clear insight into what the U.S. intentions towards the Soviet Union actually are. Noam is absolutely right in saying that at the moment the aim is not only to limit the Soviet Union but to really break it up and turn it into the third world so that it can be exploited.

Hadi: You both talked a little bit about the resources of the Middle East, namely the oil. Now the American

consumers do not get more than 7 percent of their oil from
the Middle East. Can you elaborate on the interests of the
U.S. administration and the economics of oil in that respect?

Chomsky: If the United States did not get one drop
of oil from the Middle East it would still pursue the same
policies. In fact, until 1968 the United States dominated
the Western hemisphere, where the major producers of
the world are. At that time it was an exporter of oil yet it
followed exactly the same policy as it does now when it
imports some oil. The point is: whoever has their hand on
the spigot that controls the flow of oil can influence the
rest of the world. If the United States had all the oil it
needed it would still want to control Middle East oil,
because that is the way you control the rest of the world.
That is the way you influence Europe and Japan, the
major rivals of the United States, and that is one of the
ways you insure that the third world stays under control.
It is just an important lever of world control.

The United States also needs the profits from oil
production, now delivered indirectly through the local
managers. If they suddenly discovered a resource in Idaho
which removed the need for foreign oil, that would not
change anything.

Hadi: We've discussed oil and U.S. government policy. How does the U.S. oil industry figure in this?

Chomsky: The U.S. oil industry works very closely
with the tiny elites that have been given the right to
exploit Arab oil for their own interests. Actually, I think
that in this particular crisis, the oil companies are probably against the war. The oil companies are usually against
wars; wars don't do them any good. They may like the
threat of war, which allows for price increases, but they
do not like war itself. It is very dangerous and they are
very concerned. Why? One possible outcome of this war

might be that the United States will find itself in a war
with the whole Arab world and it will be driven out of the
Middle East. If this happened, U.S. rivals—Germany and
Japan—will be perfectly happy to walk in and take it over
and that will reduce the United States to a second-class
power. This would be very harmful to the oil industry and
oil executives can see that. They are not fools and they do
not want this conflict to develop to that point.

On the other hand, there is a contradiction between
supporting the oil industry and being number 1. As Eqbal
said, if you want to stay number 1, you win a victory by
military force. If there is a diplomatic settlement, and
Saddam Hussein pulls out of Kuwait, the United States
gains nothing from it. The United States has no particular
power in the area of diplomacy; its power is in the arena
of force. It wants a forcible settlement to show that force
works and force is the way you rule the world. We are the
ones who have the force so there has to be a military
victory. The oil companies have more parochial concerns:
how to make profits and keep business going and so on.
For them the war will not do it, though they are delighted
to make profits from the higher prices.

Ahmad: I wish to emphasize the point that Noam is
making. Oil is an instrument of power, it is not an economic necessity for the United States. If there is a negotiated settlement to this crisis, the Palestinians will be
gainers, the Arab people will be gainers. Even Iraq will be
a gainer and imperialism will be a loser. The longer this
crisis lasts the more imperialism gains.

Chomsky: Right. Take a look who is opposing a
negotiated settlement, the United States and Britain.

Ahmad: And Israel.

Chomsky: Of the major powers, it is the United
States and Britain. Israel just wants the Iraqis destroyed.

Hadi: If we can also talk about Israel's role within U.S. policy in the region *vis a vis* the Palestinian situation and now the Gulf. Israel has been the country that is really pushing the United States, urging it to go to war. While it does not shape U.S. policy, it urges—

Chomsky: It urges, but we should not exaggerate Israel's power. Its influence is not zero, but if the U.S. ever decides that it's in its own best interest to turn against Israel, it will do so.

Hadi: But you have talked and written about Israel as a strategic ally.

Chomsky: The strategic alliance started in the late 1950s, and it was directed against Nasser. In the early 1970s, we recall that Nasser was virtually at war with Saudi Arabia over Yemen. Israel was regarded by U.S. intelligence as a barrier against Nasserite pressure on the oil-producing monarchies. Israeli troops may have been fighting alongside the Saudi Arabian forces. Documents on that have yet to be released but there seems to be evidence to that effect. Certainly Israel was regarded as a barrier to Nasser. Now in 1967, Israel succeeded in crushing Egypt and Syria and that was a big benefit. The United States was very strongly in support of Israel. Nasser was the radical nationalist, he was causing problems. Israel got rid of him. My strong impression is that Saudi Arabia was probably very much in favor of the Israeli victory.

After that period, a tacit alliance developed between Israel, Saudi Arabia and Iran. Iran was then the guardian of the Gulf under the Shah. It was Iran which sent troops to Dhofar [in the Sultanate of Oman] to fight with the British and Jordanians against the rebellion and so on. Iran was techncally at war with Saudi Arabia, but still there was an alliance. And there was an Israeli-Iranian alliance as well. That was described quite openly by the

Senate's major specialist on oil and the Middle East, Henry Jackson. He openly talked about a tripartite alliance between Israel, Iran and Saudi Arabia. The alliance between Israel and Iran was later revealed after the fall of the Shah. With the fall of the monarchy in Saudi Arabia, maybe similar evidence will appear showing an Israeli-Saudi Arabian alliance. But there is little doubt that that relationship existed.

Israel has been regarded as a base for American power and a potential threat against radical nationalism. Right now, Israel's interests and U.S. interests conflict in a narrow sense: Israel wants the United States to go to war to destroy Iraq. But it also wants the United States to be in conflict with the Arab states. It does not like the alliance between the U.S. and Saudi Arabia and there is a conflict. This is one of the reasons why the United States is trying to keep Israel from doing anything. If Israel got involved, that would break up the fragile alliance the United States has with sectors in the Arab world. On the other hand, if the United States attacks, if the war in the Gulf turns into a conflict between the United States and the Arab world as it may, Israel will be a base for U.S. action. Israel serves, just as it did in 1958, as the one reliable pro-Western power and a military power that the United States can count on to do what it wants. Israel is an efficient mercenary state.

Hadi: Eqbal, even with the end of the Cold War, Israel can no longer use the argument that it is the linchpin for the U.S. strategy against the "Soviet threat." What role do you think it plays now in U.S. strategy?

Ahmad: First of all, I think that we should remind ourselves that no serious-minded American policymaker took the "Soviet threat" seriously. They always knew that the "Soviet threat" was an instrument of legitimation for American policy rather than a real threat. Therefore,

Israel's importance never hinged on the existence of that threat, and will remain. Israel is really concerned about the crisis, as Noam has said, because if there is not a war and some sort of an alliance builds up between conservative Arab states and the United States, then Israel's importance may well be diminished. On the other hand, if there is a war, it is likely to turn into a war between the Arab people and the United States, in which case the United States may find itself isolated in the Arab world and then count on Israel to be its only ally in the region. That is what the Israelis would like.

We should also keep in mind that Israel's importance in American policy increased heavily in the late 1960s and early 1970s as a result of its renewed concentration on the Middle East. Israel and Iran were chosen as the two eyes, as people say in the Pentagon, of America in the Middle East. They were the regional enforcers of the Nixon Doctrine. As a result of that promotion of Israel, the pro-Israeli lobby has also become very strong in this country. By 1990 it acquired a life of its own. So two things have to be taken into account: there is a continuity of American interests in Israel as a force for American interests; and there is also now a massive lobby which wants to keep it that way. I think it very likely that American policy toward Israel will not change.

As far as the Arabs are concerned, I do not think that we really have to look for too much evidence of Saudi or Kuwaiti complicity in America's alliance with Israel. All you have to do is to look at the money. Take a look at the increase in America's military and economic aid to Israel starting in 1968-69, and take a look at the volume of Saudi, Kuwaiti, and Gulf trade with the United States. Arab commerce with the United States has increased in direct proportion to American supplies to Israel. Given that correlation, we need not wait for documentation.

Hadi: You raised a very important issue about the

Arab world, and it raises three issues. First, the question of democracy and human rights in the region. Second, the question of economic lack of distribution of resources and wealth. And third, how does the Gulf crisis affect these two issues?

Ahmad: At the moment it is unclear, because I have not been able to detect so far a healthy response from the Arab intelligentsia towards this crisis. The Arab people have suffered so much in their pride, in humiliation, in indignity and frankly in loss of territories, that out of sheer desperation they tend to applaud every instance of triumphalism. Triumphalism is a particular disease of the desperate and the hopeless. We have a tendency to applaud heavily Saddam Hussein, applaud Hafez Assad, applaud the seizure of Beirut. Call everything a victory, instead of looking reality in the face and saying, "this what we need to do." So in the absence of responses by Arab intelligentsia, I am unable to say something very hopeful about the prospects of human rights.

However, there has been a yearning towards democracy which began to be expressed in the last two and a half to three years; insufficiently, but it has been expressed. There has been definite evidence of creativity which I have not seen in the Muslim world for the last 300 years. It is now evident in Arabic literature, in Arab poetry, in some Arab art. So, for the first time, there are beginnings of creative activity. Unfortunately, a lot of it is being carried out from abroad. It is not in Cairo, it is not in Damascus. It is often in Paris, in London, which is very disturbing in some ways.

Finally, I think that even the conservative regimes are beginning to feel threatened by the very monsters they have created: the monster of the fundamentalist movement on the one hand; and the monster of aggressive statism on the other. The Saddam monster and the fundamentalist monster. Maybe we will learn something from it; maybe this is going to give us pause. But I am saddened to notice that the evidence is very grim.

Hadi: Where does the intifada fit into all of this?

Ahmad: The tragedy of the intifada is among the people that talk so much about the unity of culture, unity of Arab history, and unity of Arab emotion. One of the most unique events of modern history—the intifada—did not move the Arab world. We have entered the third year of the intifada. In the annals of the history of resistance there are very few examples like this, in which an essentially unarmed people are occupied by a very ruthless and armed force that aims not at the exploitation of the occupied population but at its exclusion and expulsion. The intifada has managed to stand up and sustain resistance for two and a half years. But it had no effect in Egypt or Saudi Arabia, very little in Syria, and very little effect in Iraq. I consider this a great tragedy.

Chomsky: What about further away like Algeria?

Ahmad: It has basically produced a right-wing response. Only the rightists have profited so far. I think that we have very serious problems to discuss with our people in the Arab world.

Hadi: I want to address the question of solutions and visions of the future. Where do you both see the possibilities for ending the crisis with the least possible loss of human lives?

Chomsky: That depends whether this crisis is ended by diplomacy or by the use of force. If the crisis is to be ended by diplomacy, of course there will be linkage. There must be and there should be. A diplomatic settlement of the Iraqi aggression in Kuwait has to be part of a regional settlement. That is what diplomacy and a diplomatic settlement entails; it deals with relevant issues.

You deal with relevant issues and try to solve them. In this respect, Saddam Hussein's first comment, around August 12—that there should be a regional settlement involving Kuwait, Syria in Lebanon, and Israel in the occupied territories and Lebanon—is a perfectly reasonable comment.

The United States is strongly opposed to linkage on the grounds that aggression cannot be rewarded. That is nonsense, because other kinds of aggressions are rewarded all the time. Turkey's aggression in Cyprus is rewarded; Israel's aggression is rewarded; Morocco's aggression in the Western Sahara is rewarded; U.S. aggression in Panama is rewarded. Refusing to reward aggression is not an American principle. The issue is: can there be a negotiated diplomatic settlement or do we win by force? When the United States opposes linkage and says we want to win by force, it is not because negotiated settlement is impossible but because we want the power of U.S. military force to decide the conflict and do not want to negotiate a settlement.

Hadi: Do you think that they are opting for a military solution?

Chomsky: I do not know; there is opposition to war too. There are powerful interests in the United States that perceive that war could be extremely harmful to U.S. interests. So there is an internal conflict. But so far the only real alternative to force is diplomacy and the United States has instantaneously blocked every hint of a diplomatic settlement. It is like a reflex reaction. Somebody hints at a diplomatic settlement, there is a sharp reaction from Washington saying absolutely not. And the media go along.

Now with regard to Israel and Palestine, the United States has always been opposed to a diplomatic settlement. It is opposed to diplomacy in the Arab-Israeli con-

flict and it has been opposed to it since 1970. Again, there
was a split among U.S. policymakers back around 1970.
It was sort of symbolized by the conflict between Secretary
of State Rogers and National Security Adviser Kissinger.
But it was a deeper split than that. Kissinger wanted a
stalemate, no political settlement. Rogers made a proposal, the Rogers plan, which in fact was everybody else's
proposal. Sadat made a similar proposal aiming to get
beyond the stalemate in 1971. Kissinger won out on the
internal conflict on the basis that Israel is our strategic
ally and a political settlement would not reinforce this
role. But whatever the reasons, that position won out and
it remains. The United States has blocked every move
towards a political settlement ever since. It has vetoed
Security Council resolutions, it voted against General
Assembly resolutions.

Right now, the United States is supporting the
Shamir plan. Incidently, the terms of the Shamir plan
have never been published in the United States. Despite
it being official U.S. policy, the only publication of it to my
knowledge is in an article of mine in an obscure magazine.
The reason for it not being published in the major media
is that, if you write those terms out, they are so horren-
dous that people will explode.

The terms of the U.S. position, the Shamir plan, are
that there already is a Palestinian state, and that Jordan
is the Palestinian state. There can be no second Palestinian state. That's point number one. Point number two is
that there can be no change in the status of Gaza, Judea
and Samaria except in accordance with the guidelines of
the Israeli government, which of course rule out any
Palestinian self-determination. Notice that there is no
mention even made of the Golan Heights. The third point
is: there can be no negotiations with the PLO, which
means that the Palestinians are not even allowed to
choose their own representatives for eventual negotiations. Fourth, in that framework, there could be what is

called free elections under Israeli military occupation
with the whole Arab intelligentsia and leadership rotting
away in jail. Those are the conditions for free elections. If
those terms were written up, everybody would laugh. So,
therefore, the media have literally not reported what is
consistent U.S. policy.

The whole talk of negotiations with the PLO was just
a trick. The PLO fell for it because they are not very bright,
in my opinion. The United States had gotten itself in a
diplomatic corner in 1988. It had tried to reject diplomacy
at every conceivable turn and it was becoming the laugh-
ingstock of the world. So finally the United States did a
typical diplomatic maneuver that you do when you are
trapped: you pretend that the opponent has capitulated
and accepted your terms. Then you say: OK, it is my terms
that worked and the American terms are exactly these.

In the first meeting of the negotiations—the transcript was leaked and published both in Egypt and in
Israel—the U.S. position was twofold. First, there will be
no international conference, because if there is an international conference there will be pressure for a political
settlement and the United States is against a political
settlement. Secondly, the PLO must call off the intifada,
these riots against the state of Israel which we regard as
terrorism. Call off the intifada and the international conference; then maybe we will talk to you. In other words,
now we are back where we were before—we do nothing
like we have done nothing before. That is the American
position.

This purpose of the negotiations was expressed very
clearly by Yitzhak Rabin, who was defense minister at the
time. Rabin had an interview with members of Peace
Now—it is sort of mainstream peace group—in February
1989, right after the negotiations had started. It was
reported in the Hebrew press. He told them: don't worry
about the negotiations. They are not a problem because
the Americans are keeping the negotiations at a low level

and the purpose of the negotiations is to give us a year or more to crush the Palestinians by force. Then Rabin added: they will be broken. Now, the Peace Now leaders made no objections to this other than tactical ones. Some members did not think it was going to work. If there were any other objections, they were not reported.

The negotiation strategy of the United States did work. The Israelis had a year or more to use force and to institute rigid totalitarian control which probably does not exist to this extent anywhere else in the world. Ultimately, you can crush an unarmed civilian population and that was the tactic employed. And the PLO fell for it. As with the Arab world, the PLO also did not really direct resources to support the people fighting the occupation. In any case, the U.S./Israeli tactic was used because the United States does not want a diplomatic settlement to the Palestinian problem. They want Israel to be strong.

Israel is a strategic ally and a mercenary state—by now it is a mercenary state used worldwide by the United States. Other countries hire terrorists. The United States is a big power and we do not kid around with individual terrorists. We hire terrorist states. So when it runs terrorist operations, it has networks with Taiwan, Israel, Saudi Arabia (which does the bankrolling). Take support for the contras. That was a very complex terrorist operation. The United States did not just hire a Carlos; they hired Taiwan, Argentinean Nazis. Saudi Arabia paid some of the cost and the Sultan of Brunei paid more. Israel brought arms and training.

This use of terrorist states is a big operation. Israel is a very significant and very efficient mercenary state, and as long as military conflicts continue in the Middle East, it is going to be dependent on the United States for its survival. Therefore, it is dependable and is going to continue being dependable because of its dependence. When the Iran-Contra operations were finally partially exposed, one government official described Israel as just another federal agency that we turn to when we want to get something done. That is basically correct. Saudi Arabia is another federal agency that we turn to when we want to fund some terrorist operation. That is part of the U.S. global system.

The Palestinians, on the other hand, have nothing to offer the United States. They do not have military force, they do not have resources. Since no question of democracy or self-determination or human rights has even a marginal role in policy formation, Palestinians are basically powerless.

Ahmad: To add to what Noam has already said, we must ask, who is going to push for linkage? The people who are supposed to push for linkage are not pushing it. Saudi Arabia is not pushing for linkage. The Emirates of the Gulf are not pushing for it. Egypt is not pushing for linkage. Syria is not pushing for linkage. So the posture of the Arab states is not to mention linkage, perhaps with the exception of King Hussein of Jordan in whose interest it is to push for linkage. As Noam has already mentioned, the reason the United States has rejected linkage is that they want to keep Israel as the primate of *pax Americana* in the Middle East.

Hadi: Do you think there will be a military solution?

Ahmad: I am not sure of that. I am not sure that there will be a military solution. There are only two and a half forces in the world at the moment which are calling for a military solution. One is the executive branch of the American government, perhaps backed up by a portion of the Pentagon, which wants to keep its dividends in war rather than giving them to peaceful domestic programs. Second is the Israeli government and its supporters in the United States. Perhaps you can add to it the other half portion, namely the government of Kuwait and perhaps Britain. I am not sure of Britain so much, because it is so divided. Against that you have more or less the array of other forces which oppose a military solution. That is why I think our job is to find every possible way to pressure Saddam Hussein to make the linkage and make it consistently and pressure the United States to negotiate, because negotiations will then include linkage.

"From We Pay, You Fight to You Pay, We Fight"

Interview with Abbas Nasrawi and Naseer Aruri by Rabab Hadi

November 17, 1990

In asking questions of Nasrawi and Aruri which are similar to those asked of Chomsky and Ahmad, Hadi reveals a growing consensus about the nature of U.S. policy in the Middle East, while capturing the richness of different perspectives.

Hadi: What is your assessment of current U.S. policy towards the region in terms of the Gulf and of Palestine? Does this policy mark a departure from past policies or a continuation?

Nasrawi: I don't think that it marks any major departure. I think it is consistent with past U.S. policies both in the region and towards the third world. The U.S. has always had its foreign policy objectives in the region very clearly defined. One, to control oil. Two, to protect the Gulf sheikhdoms and principalities of states. Three, to continue its strategic relationship with Israel. Four, it would like to continue its control over oil as a leverage *vis a vis* its economic competitors, primarily Japan and Western Europe. On all these counts, there has been no departure. And the underlying force is that the United States does not wish to be challenged by any third world nationalist movement. The Gulf situation was perceived by the United States as a challenge by a third world nationalist leader.

Aruri: I agree entirely with Abbas: there really has not been a major departure in policy toward the Middle East. The American policy since the Second World War has aimed to maintain hegemonic control over the region. They opposed every single movement, every nationalist movement that aimed to transfer the decision regarding the destiny of the area from abroad and from puppets to genuine nationalist people. This is really what America has been opposing.

If we look at the history of the past 40 years or more, we see that every single American president, with the exception of two, have doctrines named after them. The Truman doctrine, the Carter doctrine, the Nixon doctrine, all the way up to the Reagan doctrine and now I think that there is a Bush doctrine as well. Yet all these different doctrines have one aim in common: to prevent people in the region from unifying around a program that would take this area away from neocolonialism.

But what we are seeing right now is somewhat different. The differences lie in the tactics and means used to accomplish the objectives. The objectives are really the same. Take, for example, the Nixon doctrine and the Bush doctrine. I look at the Bush doctrine as a reversal of the Nixon doctine. The Nixon doctrine was premised on the notion that America would supply the hose and the water and the Arabs and the Iranians and the Israelis would supply the firemen. But the Iranian fireman was overtaken by the blaze. And then people like Zbigniew Brzezinski, who was national security adviser under Carter, say we really cannot overstuff third world leaders with weapons and technology that they cannot use. Instead, we need to be able to intervene directly. This gave rise to the Rapid Deployment Force that Brzezinski and others developed in 1977 which came into fruition in 1990. The Bush doctrine reverses this in the sense that the Saudis and the Gulf people pay and the Americans are the firemen. So it is the exact reverse, but the same objective of controlling third world countries in a neocolonial context and destroying their nationalist movements.

Nasrawi: It was said that the Nixon doctrine could be summarized by saying "we pay, you fight." The Bush doctrine reversed that by saying "you pay, we fight." As far as the Soviet Union is concerned, it ceases to be a superpower. In this particular situation it has acted as a junior partner in the whole effort.

Hadi: Naseer, what do you think about this? There is the end of the Cold War and the relaxation of tension internationally—or presumed to be—and then here we see a major crisis happening that not only threatens the region but the world over. How do you see the role of the Soviet Union in the post-Cold War era? Some say the Soviets are no longer acting as a deterrent to U.S. aggression. Do you agree?

Aruri: Absolutely. It is no longer a deterrent force. It seems to be lacking the willingness and the capacity to act as a deterrent. Had the Soviet Union been able to act as a deterrent, as it did during the Cold War, I think that the countervailing system would have worked. But in this era, the Americans really had a green light. What is more disturbing is that the Soviet Union has spoken about the possibility of the use of force—not exactly in the same context as the Americans do—but nevertheless, they have talked about it. Shevardnadze spoke about it, Gorbachev did and Primakov did. Even though, in all fairness, one has to say that the Soviet Union has been saying that we did not exhaust the remedies. But what is important here is that they know the bottom line, at the end of the road, at the end of the day, if Saddam Hussein does not withdraw from Kuwait then the use of force is going to happen. That is a first for the Soviet Union in the Security Council.

There are basic differences between the Soviets and the United States with regard to the legal basis for the use of force. The Americans are going on the basis of article 51; the Soviets would like to go on the basis of article 42. Fifty-one is about self-defense, under which the Americans actually reinterpret international law and say that they have the right to use force, which is ridiculous. The Soviets disagree. According to the Soviets, if the U.S. wants to use force, they have to revive the Military Staff Committee, which has the five permanent members of the Security Council. This would mean the U.S. would not be the leader of the attacking force. It would be the Chinese, and the Soviets, and the Americans, and so forth. But it seems to me that the Soviets are acting more like North than East; they are part of the North.

Hadi: So you would say that the conflict has been transformed from East-West to North-South. In addition to transforming conflicts from East-West to North-South, the close of the Cold War has been accompanied in the United States by many forces pushing for a peace dividend—the demand that money be taken out of the military budget and spent on social programs. How do you see that being affected by the Gulf crisis?

Nasrawi: In the process of ending the Cold War, the military doctrines and Pentagon thinking shifted from confrontations between the West and the East to confrontation or potential confrontations between the North and the South. Prior to the crisis, it was expected that the budget of the Defense Department was going to be reduced. The crisis in the Gulf played into the hands of those who opposed any reduction in the budget and provided them, unfortunately, with the pretext for maintaining or increase the budget because there are going to continue to be flashpoints, trouble spots, and regional third world conflicts.

Aruri: I think that this may have been one of the motives that was behind Bush's decision to mobilize. Although one has to think of it as a multi-dimensional issue, this is certainly one important consideration. It was crucial to be able to take the argument that "now is the time for the peace dividend" away from some legislators. I think that there really has been a thrust in the U.S. Congress. I believe that there was momentum building up for the peace dividend as the Cold War ended and it made sense to redirect our priorities and begin to channel resources into social services and to set our backyard in order. But, of course, Bush and his supporters do not wish to admit this was a motivating factor.

Hadi: In looking at the factors behind Bush's Gulf policy, we have touched on the need to crush movements aimed at taking the region out from under its neocolonial existence, the inability to rely on local forces such as was done with Iran in the days of the Shah, and the need to circumvent calls for the peace dividend. What about the factor of oil? Middle East oil accounts for between 7 and 10 percent of U.S. consumption. Yet, policymakers have enunciated the importance of oil many times. How does it fit in?

Nasrawi: In the first half of 1990, the United States was getting only about 4 percent of its oil consumption from Kuwait and Iraq combined. Now, it should be kept in mind that the United States imports oil regularly. But it does not come from the Middle East alone. It comes from Mexico, Venezuela and other parts of the world. The question of oil goes beyond the day-to-day consumption needs of the American society. Oil is a vehicle of control. Oil is a leverage, the control of which could be used to achieve economic and political objectives either within the region or outside the region. There is also another dimension for oil that has be kept in mind: that is, when you raise the price of oil internationally, you are going to unfreeze the price of oil in this country. The United States is the largest oil-producing country in the world. Therefore, there would be a great deal of economic benefits that would accrue to the oil-producing states in this country.

Furthermore, as the price of oil goes up, so will the cash revenues of the U.S. treasury. It has been estimated that this year alone, as a result of these price increases, the U.S. treasury will collect $20 billion more in taxes. So there is also the domestic factor—the domestic politics and the domestic economic interests—that are involved. The American Ambassador to Baghdad told Saddam Hussein that there are many people in the United States who would like to see the price of oil set at $25 a barrel when OPEC had just agreed to set it at $21. That speaks a great deal about the economic benefits that she had in mind and what interest groups from the United States she was representing.

Aruri: I want to focus for a moment on the Rapid Deployment Force and to emphasize that the American invasion—I do not want to call it intervention—is something that has been planned for since the inception of the Force. It was organized for this very purpose. When the military bases were built in Saudi Arabia, they were not built to accommodate a Saudi military infrastructure. The key word in the Pentagon at that time was "over-building." It was something that has been contemplated for a long time.

Hadi: How is Israel involved in the evolution of these events? Israel has been talked about in the media as the "wild card." Others have said Israel's strategic importance to the United States after the end of the Cold War, and prior to the Gulf intervention has been in decline. How do you see Israel right now—before and after the Gulf crisis—where does it fit in U.S. strategy?

Aruri: There is a strong body of opinion that Israel will cease to be the strategic asset that it has been. Here, strategic asset means being an attack dog. And now with the Soviet Union gone, there is essentially no one to attack. I do not really see it that way, because the Soviet

Union has never really been the real enemy throughout
the post-Second World War period. The unstated enemy
has been Arab nationalism; the stated enemy has been the
Soviet Union. And now with the Soviets gone, the bogy-
man is going to be Islam; it's going to be radical Arabs,
tyrants and people like that. And Saddam somehow per-
sonifies all these things, even though he is not Islamic. I
think that the United States does still see the importance
of the strategic relationship which was concretized between the years 1983 and 1988. And I would say that in
the case of a war, should the United States decide to go to
war, you can be sure that Israel will be involved in the
preparations because of the pre-positioning and the stock-
piling that these arrangements provide for.

I do not really buy the argument that Israel will
cease to be a big asset and that the assets are now going
to be Egypt, Syria and so on. The United States knows
that it cannot rely on those Arab regimes. Today they are
here, tomorrow they may not be. Secondly, the United
States has contempt for people like Syria's Assad. They
can deal with him in terms of a temporary convergence of
interests, but not in terms of strategic alliances.

Hadi: When you addressed the question of Israel, you
talked about the nature of the Arab regimes, which the Gulf
crisis definitely brings out, of human rights, of democracy
and democratization, of economic and social justice, fair
distribution of the region's resources. Please expand on that.

Nasrawi: One of the major tragedies of the Arab
state system over the last 25 years, in the aftermath of the
1967 defeat, has been exactly that—to shut out public
participation. I mean participation of the masses in the
decision-making process through their organizations, institutions, voting and things of that sort. It goes without
saying that public input into decisionmaking is extremely
essential to democracy and justice.

Rulers, regardless of where they are, whether they are in the Arab world, Eastern Europe, or in Latin America, are stumbling from one crisis to another. Political and economic decisions are becoming a matter of life and death. So the question of countervailing forces, checks and balances input from various groups, advice and so on, are all elements of decisionmaking which become very important. As for the distribution of income and wealth in the Arab region, we have to speak about that at two levels. At the social level, we have to make sure that for people at large there are benefits from the income and wealth that accrue to that particular nation. There is also the question of income distribution and wealth distribution between various countries. If you look at the Arab map, the per capita income ranges from $400 for countries like Sudan and Mauritania to $16,000 or $17,000 for countries like the United Arab Emirates. This simply is not a tenable situation. If these countries are separate from each other, then one could look at it from that perspective. But as long as one talks about the Arab League, Arab proliferation, Arab integration, Arab unity, Arab nationalism, we simply cannot leave the decision of the transfer of capital in the hands of the few or the governments. We simply cannot have that done on a bilateral basis: you provide the money when you approve of the program—the political program—of this government or that group. The disparity in the distribution of income and wealth among these countries and within these countries has been an important factor in the destabilization, which elicited, unfortunately, a repressive response from these regimes.

Aruri: Well, I think that how the movement for democracy will be affected will depend on how the crisis is resolved. I think that if a war takes place, the devastation and the dislocation and the possible disappearance of states are going to really overwhelm those thinking in terms of democracy.

Yet, I keep in mind that the case for democracy right

now is very compelling in the Arab world. Just to give you one small example, if Kuwait had democracy and Iraq had democracy, they would have done better. Kuwait crumbled in half an hour. If Kuwait had democracy, it would mean that, instead of having six people participate in making decisions, you have a million people. But with decisionmaking concentrated in the hands of so few, they folded in half an hour. And if Iraq had democracy, if Saddam Hussein consulted and so on, he might have been told by his advisers that he is not to miscalculate, there is a new world order, at least the rules of the game are very fluid and they're being transformed at present.

A total war will focus people in the area on survival. A generation might pass before any sort of political reconstruction took place. A diplomatic settlement would give the movement which is underway a better chance. I think that there will be a real push towards democracy and towards human rights.

What is interesting, if you look at the lineup of forces now in the Gulf, they are anti-U.S. and pro-U.S. The pro-U.S. are those states which have no democracy whatsoever, siding with the great democracy of the world, so to speak. The anti-U.S. countries include Tunisia where there is real progress towards democracy. In Jordan, there is also movement toward more political participation. Algeria is going to have elections for the first time, even though the lame duck president there knows that he is not going to be elected. Then there is Yemen, where strides towards participation are taking place. Similar moves are being made by the Palestinians as well.

Hadi: You talked about alternatives for peace. What are the possibilities? The United States is opting for a military solution; meanwhile, there are many initiatives coming from the region talking about linkage. Do you think there should be a linkage between Iraqi occupation of Kuwait and Israeli occupation of Palestine?

Nasrawi: I think that the question of linkage is not only legitimate, it is overdue. If one were to look at the UN Security Council resolutions with respect to Israeli occupation and with respect to Iraqi invasion of Kuwait, one would see the wording is the same over the years. As we all know, the United States has opted to neglect the resolution of the Palestine issue over the last 23 years. In fact, the United States has supported Israeli policies militarily, financially, politically, and diplomatically. So there is a double standard, a double morality. So the question of linkage is natural and compelling. I do believe linkage to be in the interest of the entire region and certainly the world.

Aruri: I think linkage is a reality, no question about it. Not only has it been acknowledged by those who claim it does not exist, but there is a logic in the world nowadays of the need to deal comprehensively with the outstanding issues in regional conflicts. And if we look at many regional conflicts, we learn that resolution is possible. I am talking about Afghanistan, Cambodia, Southern Africa, Central America and so on and so forth. Resolution isn't necessarily to my satisfaction, but at least the concept of resolution is there. In the Middle East we have to argue for resolution, which is very, very strange. Resolution is possible, but is blocked by outright rejectionism on the part of Israel and on the part of the United States. But linkage is a reality today. This is made clear by U.S. actions. It wants to maintain its hegemony, which is why it supports the Israeli occupation on the one hand and is challenging the Iraqi occupation on the other. Hegemony is the key and so the two things are linked. In fact, I would say three things are linked, because the Middle East has three conflicts; Lebanon, the Gulf, and the Palestinians. I think that the majority of the world today recognizes the fact that they all have to be dealt with comprehensively.

Taking a Stand
Against the Double Standard

Jeanne Butterfield

*Because of time constraints, this article was submit-
ted as written answers to Rabab Hadi's questions. In this
tour de force, Butterfield captures the essence of the U.S.
role in the Persian Gulf crisis, makes the connections
between militarism and deepening domestic problems,
and points out the basis for believing that organizing can
bring the war to a close.*

How is it that the United States cannot abide an
Iraqi occupation for more than a few months, when it has
tolerated if not supported Israeli occupation of Palestinian
territory for 23 years? How is it that Bush maintains that
there is no room for negotiations without an unconditional
withdrawal of Iraqi forces from Kuwait, when Israeli forces
continue to occupy the West Bank and Gaza Strip while
the United States tries to coax the Israeli government to
the negotiating table? How is it that the United States
urges the UN Security Council to impose sanctions hastily
against Iraq, when it vetoes even mild censure of the
Israeli occupation and certainly would never countenance
sanctions as a form of pressure against that occupation?

The U.S. double standard is clear. And Bush's rationale for war in the Gulf remains unconvincing. Bush's
"line in the sand" has nothing to do with fighting aggression or preserving the sovereignty of nations, ideals which
the United States has betrayed time and again, from
Grenada and Panama to the West Bank and Gaza. The
line in the sand is oil company profits and U.S. control

over world oil supplies. Nothing more, nothing less. It is not a line which the U.S. people are willing to defend with their lives and their blood.

United States' strategic interests in the Gulf have always been about the control of oil. In the old Cold War context, the United States could cloak this interest in the guise of "containment"—containing the Soviet threat, containing communism. Now, in the new world order, the United States is concerned with continuing to maintain its dominance, its hegemony. But its economy is no longer as strong as it used to be. The United States cannot buy influence with foreign aid in the way it used to. It has to resort to military force directly in order to get what it wants. And what the United States wants is to protect its place in the new tri-polar world order. What better way to ensure that than with a stranglehold on oil? It's not the supply of oil to the United States that the Bush administration is concerned about. It is concerned about the control of the pricing and distribution of oil upon which Europe and Japan depend. Less than 5 percent of the 15 million barrels of oil that the United States consumes each day comes from Iraq and Kuwait. In fact, the oil that it would lose as a result of a lengthy Iraqi occupation of Kuwait could easily be made up by modest efforts at energy conservation. The savings from a three-mile-per-gallon increase in auto efficiency would more than compensate for the loss of imported Kuwaiti oil.

The stability of the Saudi regime and its compliance with U.S. interests has been a priority of U.S. foreign policy ever since the 1930s. Saddam Hussein is a dangerous man not because he would overrun Saudi oil fields and hold half the world's oil supply hostage. He is dangerous to the United States because he threatens to upset the entire hierarchy of Arab ruling elites and U.S.-based multinationals and their control of production and marketing of world oil. This is carried out at the expense of the Arab elites' own people and the Arab world as a whole.

Control of this oil will ensure the U.S. place as a world power in the new tri-polar world order in the decades ahead. It is this strategic vision which is driving U.S. intervention in the Gulf.

On the question of how Israel fits into U.S. strategy and policy given the Gulf crisis, there are differences among the U.S. ruling elite about the continuing value of Israel as a strategic ally. Certainly in terms of the oil card, Israel has no value. And in terms of military assistance and the forward placement of military equipment and supplies, Israel would very quickly lose its value if the United States is about to establish a permanent base in Saudi Arabia, a goal of U.S. planners for several decades. But Israel still has strategic value as the defender of U.S. interests in the region and the U.S. role in the world, because Israel is certainly still a client state and still the largest recipient of U.S. foreign aid.

I think that the scenario recently outlined by Francis Boyle and James Ridgeway is plausible. That is, the United States would be happy to disarm Saddam Hussein, negotiate a peace treaty between Syria and Israel in which Syria gets back the Golan Heights and Israel gets southern Lebanon, and the Palestinians are expelled in large numbers to Jordan, perhaps even toppling the Jordanian monarchy. The "Jordan is Palestine" scenario is still an acceptable one to the United States, I believe, so long as stability in the region is assured.

The implications of the Gulf crisis for democracy and human rights in the region could be positive. The Gulf crisis is such a crisis to the United States because it represents a potentially vast destabilizing conflict in the region. If Saddam Hussein sparks increased resistance to the Arab regimes by their own people, if the Palestinian question is linked in the eyes of the world community to resolution of the Gulf crisis, if the undemocratic and harshly repressive nature of the Kuwaiti, Saudi and Iraqi regimes is exposed, and if alignment with the U.S. military project sparks dissent among the people of Egypt and Syria, then the forces of democracy and human freedom in the region will have gained a great deal by this crisis. We may see some major changes in the Middle East in the years ahead.

Turning to the question of linkage, it is not one that Saddam Hussein alone has posed. It is posed by the very nature of the U.S. double standard in its actions in the region. The very fact that the United States has used the UN resolutions to pressure Iraq, poses the question in the minds of many about why the United States has opposed such resolutions when it comes to Israel. Support of sanctions against Iraq by many people gives us a major opening to raise the possibility of sanctions against Israel. The very fact that most people would rather see peace negotiations than war gives us a major opportunity to raise the question of an international peace conference to resolve the Israeli/Palestinian conflict. "Linkage" is not subjectively posed by some individuals; it is objectively posed by the actual situation in the Middle East.

I don't believe war was inevitable in the Gulf. However, it is largely up to the U.S. peace movement to stop it. Many sectors of U.S. society are beginning to realize that war might not be in their interest. The friends and families of military personnel, national church leaders, peace and solidarity organizations, grassroots community organizations of women, tenants, people of color, and a few enlisted men and women themselves are beginning to speak out against a war in the Middle East. Certain sectors of the government, conservative businesspeople, some U.S. congresspeople, even the *Wall Street Journal,* are beginning to think that war might not be good for business and might not pull the United States out of the recession it is in. The domestic economic costs will be high. The casualties and resulting political costs will be higher still.

The price tag for the U.S. Gulf deployment is estimated at $15 billion for 1990 alone. Some legislators have talked about the necessity of a war tax to pay for continued deployment and war in the Middle East. The U.S. defense budget is at its highest level ever, $296 billion. And the deficit reduction package has targetted working people for higher taxes and reduced social services, while the rich continue to benefit from the Reagan tax revolution which cut their tax rate from 70 percent to 28 percent. The budget cuts necessary in the next 5 years to make up the $500 billion reduction package required by law will come from Medicare, from farm subsidies, from excise taxes, and from continued cuts in job training, food stamps, and day care, cuts which are guaranteed to drive millions more U.S. people into poverty and homelessness. War will only produce bigger deficits, and will benefit no one but the defense industry, arms manufacturers and oil companies which will profit from the price gouging at the gas tank.

People are beginning to realize this. Bush's explanations for war—that we're fighting for oil, or against "naked aggression," or for American jobs, or against Saddam's nuclear capability—has not stopped anti-war sentiment from being expressed in more and more vocal ways. There have been teach-ins and town meetings against war. There are many military people refusing to go to the Gulf. There have been fairly large local demonstrations, and national demonstrations in Washington. We're much further ahead than we were in this stage of the Vietnam War. I think we will stop the war. We have to. For ourselves and for the people of the Middle East.

Power Projection in the Middle East

Maintaining Control at Any Cost

Sheila Ryan

What are the defining features of U.S. Middle East policy as it shifts from the containment policy of the last 45 years to the "new world order"? By tracing the history of U.S. relations with Iraq and neighboring states, Ryan reveals the essential continuities and striking differences between the Cold War era and today.

What responsibility does the United States have in the creation of the Gulf crisis? A review of diplomatic initiatives just prior to the crisis may shed some light. A further review of U.S. military policy and aims reveal a power projection in the region which made a crisis such as the one in the Persian Gulf highly probable.

On July 25, 1990, U.S. Ambassador April Glaspie told Saddam Hussein that the United States had "no opinion" on border disputes between Arab states, such as the Iraqi-Kuwaiti dispute. She assured Saddam Hussein, irate that Kuwait is over-pumping from the Rumaila oil field—from which both countries draw—and pushing down oil prices, that "some Texas oilmen" in the United States would be pleased to see prices rise.[1] The Iraqi president may well have interpreted Ambassador Glaspie's behavior as conveying the "winks and nods" of tacit support—particularly since Bush is a Texas oilman himself. Perhaps Saddam recalled the discreet but impor-

41

tant assistance received from the United States after its winks and nods over the Iraqi invasion of Iran, which set off eight years of war. Saddam Hussein's confidence could only have been bolstered by the ambassador's declaration that "I have a direct instruction from the President to seek better relations with Iraq."

In late June of 1990, Iraqi Ambassador Mohammed Sadiq al Mashat told the Commonwealth Club of California, "I am here on a special mission to develop a close relation between Iraq and the U.S. and to...develop a close relation between all the Arab countries and the United States..." [2]

When Secretary of Defense Dick Cheney first told the media that the United States would defend Kuwait militarily against Iraqi attack, the impression created was quickly corrected by the Pentagon's press spokesman, Pete Williams. Ambassador Glaspie's expression of neutrality was reiterated in public statements by Assistant Secretary of State for Near Eastern and South Asian Affairs, John Kelly, the last such statement coming two days before the Iraqi invasion in testimony before the House Foreign Affairs Committee.

Did the Bush administration deliberately tempt Saddam Hussein to seize Kuwait in order to provide an opportunity for a massive military response from the United States? It is too soon to attempt an answer to that question. Eventually, documents clarifying the issue may come to light. But efforts to portray administration moves before the crisis as "mistaken" are unconvincing. Secretary of State James Baker attempted to explain away the problem, stating that if he had signed a cable instructing Ambassador Glaspie to convey the message she did, it was not really meaningful because "312,000 cables" a year go out over his signature. Perhaps the decisionmakers envisioned confrontation with Iraq—possibly a confrontation short of war—which would indicate that the United States was willing to "project power" in vital areas. Whatever the

Bush administration's intentions, the crisis comes at a convenient time for the arms industry and for military strategists.

New Rationales for Military Spending in the Twilight of the Soviet Threat

The Soviet reaction to the Gulf crisis marked the end of the old rationale of containing communism which justified military spending. Less than 300 miles of Turkish or Iranian territory separate the Soviet Union from Iraq, and a U.S. attack on one of the Soviet Union's allies— Iraq— would have risked an escalation to nuclear war in the Cold War era. But the U.S. attack met with Soviet approval; it was not until after a week of intensive aerial bombardment that the Soviets raised questions over U.S. actions.

As Theodore Sorenson pointed out:

> The touchstone for our nation's security concept—the containment of Soviet military and ideological power—is gone. The primary threat cited over forty years in justification for most of our military budget, bases and overseas assistance is gone.[3]

Many domestic programs were supported, "including even financing domestic education and highway construction—in the name of outbidding, outmaneuvering or outlasting Soviet-sponsored communism," Sorenson observed. "That they are gone is a cause for rejoicing in celebration of peace and freedom," but their evaporation left a conceptual vacuum.[4] The search to create a new rationale for military spending takes place against a backdrop of economic decline in the United States, now the world's leading debtor nation with the largest trade and government budget deficits. Its market share of everything from computers to cars, in both domestic and export markets, is declining.

The specter of a declining imperial power, committed to a global military role its economy can no longer support, was outlined by Paul Kennedy in *The Rise and Fall of the Great Powers*.[5] Tracing the interaction between the economies and strategies of great powers, including Spain, the Netherlands, France, the British Empire, and United States, he discerned a cyclic pattern in which

> ...wealth is usually needed to underpin military power and military power is usually needed to acquire and protect wealth. If, however, too large a proportion of the state's resources is diverted from wealth creation and allocated instead to military purposes, then that is likely to lead to a weakening of national power over the longer term. In the same way, if a state overextends itself strategically—by say, the conquest of extensive territories or the waging of costly wars—it runs the risk that the potential benefits from external expansion may be outweighed by the great expense of it all—a dilemma which becomes acute if the nation concerned has entered a period of relative economic decline.[6]

William Hyland, editor of the prestigious journal, *Foreign Affairs*, argued that this new reality of limited economic resources would be a factor in shifting U.S. preoccupation inward:

> The Cold War was a broadly conceived struggle that gave primacy to geopolitics and military preparedness. At the outset, the United States was the most powerful nation in the world. Few questioned that it could afford the Truman Doctrine, the Marshall Plan, the rearmament of NATO, the strategic arms race, the interventions in Korea and Vietnam, or more recently, the build up of armaments in the early 1980s. For the next decade, however, ideological and military issues are likely to recede, economic factors will predominate and other issues (e.g., the environment, terrorism, drug trafficking) will grow in importance.

The United States remains the strongest world

power, indeed the only truly global power, but its resources are no longer commensurate with the mainte-
nance of the exalted position it held in the postwar
period...[7]

The voices raised on behalf of a reduction of military
spending and an increase in funding for domestic purposes included Robert McNamara, secretary of defense
from 1961-1968 and president of the World Bank from
1968-1981. He espoused a reduction in military spending
from 6 percent of the gross national product to 3 percent.[8]

What Theodore Sorenson and one sector of the political elite regarded as "a cause of rejoicing in celebration
of peace and freedom," another regarded as a matter for
deep anxiety. Colin Gray, president of National Security
Research, expressed this profound unease in a military
journal:

> ...The U.S. defense establishment is suffering from a
> crisis of uncertain higher direction that derives from the
> unanticipated measure of success of U.S., or Western,
> success in the East-West competition. The familiar ca-
> veat, "beware of your wishes, they may come true," yields
> vital insight into the current condition.[9]

Two tendencies in debate over military spending had
emerged before Bush deployed troops to Saudi Arabia.
One side argued that aside from maintaining the ability
to counter any new Soviet threat to intervene when U.S.
interests are threatened in developing countries, military
spending should decrease as the Cold War wound down.
Further, a "peace dividend" ought to be invested in the
reindustrialization of the United States, honing the competitive edge of an economy being bested by its rivals in
Germany and Japan, in the repair of its infrastructure,
including "soft" infrastructural elements like education,
and in reweaving a social fabric.

The other side urged the United States to continue
to maintain a powerful military after the departure of the

Soviet Union from superpower competition—a departure which they emphasized, could be brief. As Vice President Dan Quayle argued, a preeminent military must be available to protect U.S. interests:

> Our strategy is to maintain the peace that we now enjoy. Now, when you look at a strategy, you have to look at it in terms of the threat, you have to assess it and you have to do what is necessary. There has been a lot of discussion that, somehow with the new world we're in, the strategies that brought us to where we are now are going to radically change all of a sudden. I don't think that's going to be the case. Will they be modified to accommodate the new environment? Yes. But we're not going to throw the baby out with the bathwater. The idea of having a strong defense, the idea of having forward deployed forces and a flexible response—all of these have been very good strategies that have in fact worked...[10]

General Colin Powell, chairman of the Joint Chiefs of Staff, insisted before a Senate Committee that "We're not a bunch of Col. Blimps who can't understand the world is changing."[11] In the face of talk about military budget cuts and a "peace dividend," the military leadership began to take a new tack. In addition to the Soviets, General Powell warned of other defense obligations, including "the ongoing war in El Salvador, the coup attempt in the Philippines and the restoration of democracy in Panama," the military commitments to NATO and the bilateral military relations with Japan and South Korea, and finally our "worldwide commercial and security interests" which require a strong navy. He asserted:

> With all of these challenges and opportunities confronting our nation, it is impossible for me to believe that demobilizing or hollowing out the American military is a feasible course of action for the future. The true "peace dividend" is peace itself... Peace comes about through the maintenance of strength.[12]

The Military in the '90s
Maintaining Our Access to Their Resources

Several military figures were even more explicit than General Powell in designating other potential "threats" in the world which justified continued spending. General Carl Vuono, chief of staff of the U.S. Army, told a House Committee in May 1989 that

> Much more complex [than any peril posed by the Soviet Union] is the threat situation developing in the rest of the world. Periods of change present a fertile environment for increased instability and increased danger. In this increasingly multipolar world, we face the potential of multiple threats—from countries and factors which are becoming more sophisticated militarily and more aggressive politically." [13]

General A. M. Gray, commandant of the Marine Corps, observed:

> The international security environment is in the midst of changing from a bipolar balance to a multipolar one with polycentric dimensions. The restructuring of the international environment has the potential to create regional power vacuums that could result in instability and conflict. We cannot permit these voids to develop either through disinterest, benign neglect, or lack of capability. If we are to maintain our position as a world leader and protect our interests, we must be capable of and willing to protect our global interests. This requires that we maintain our capability to respond to likely regions of conflict. [14]

General Gray predicted that the growth of economic power of some U.S. allies would lead to their greater political and military independence and will thus "increase our requirement of forces capable of responding unilaterally."

The underdeveloped world's growing dissatisfaction over

the gap between rich and poor nations will create a fertile breeding ground for insurgencies. These insurgencies have the potential to jeopardize regional stability and our access to vital economic and military resources. This situation will become more critical as our nation and allies, as well as potential adversaries, become more and more dependent on these strategic resources. If we are to have stability in these regions, maintain access to their resources, protect our citizens abroad, defend our vital installations and deter conflict, we must maintain within our active force structure a credible military power projection capability with the flexibility to respond to conflict across the spectrum of violence throughout the globe.[15]

This emphasis on conflict in the third world began prior to the decline of the Soviet threat. During the 1980s, an extremely influential study on U.S. strategic direction was produced by a panel, chaired by Fred Iklé and Albert Wohlstetter, whose members included Henry Kissinger, Zbigniew Brzezinski, Samuel Huntington, and others. They called for a "discriminate deterrence," noting that the world is becoming less bipolar. Most of the wars in the past 40 years, and "all the wars in which the United States was involved—either directly with its forces or indirectly with military assistance—occurred in the third world."[16] According to the study, conflicts in the third world have had

an adverse cumulative effect on U.S. access to critical regions, on American credibility among allies and friends and on American self-confidence. If this cumulative effect cannot be checked or reversed in future, it will gradually undermine America's ability to defend its interest in the most vital regions, such as the Persian Gulf, the Mediterranean and the Western Pacific.[17]

To counter this deleterious impact, the study argued, the United States should reallocate its military resources so that the full range of threats—from the third world as well as the Soviet Union—could be met effectively. The term "mid-intensity" began to creep into the lexicon of the Pentagon, an early signal of the kind of war the military planners were conceiving for the third world.

The U.S. invasion of Panama, the first post-Cold War military intervention by the United States, was in certain ways a practice run for the coming operations against Iraq.[19] Strategists commented on the importance of having logistical support in place, a "receptive" airfield, and a command and control structure already operating[20]—all advantages in Panama—and learned that the night attack "was even preferable in many cases to day operations," a lesson applied in the attack on Iraq.[21]

Unlike Panama, the Middle East offers officials ready popular support at home since the "national interest" is at stake over oil. As former Secretary of Defense Caspar Weinberger, commented,

> The American people must have some kind of understanding of how important any decision to commit American forces is, and that it must be a decision required by our national interests, as for example, the Persian Gulf activities (i.e, the reflagging operations of 1987-88) were.[22]

The Preemptive Strike Against the Peace Dividend

Throughout the first half of 1990, polls indicated strong support for cutting funds from the military budget to use for a range of socially constructive purposes,[23] and lobbies for health care, education, and housing began to press for redirection of some defense budget funds.[24]

As the Senate debate on military appropriations opened in early August, Operation Desert Shield challenged the peace dividend. Minority Leader Robert Dole defended financing the B-2 bomber by declaring: "I am prepared to suggest if we are going to err, let us err on the side of being ready, being prepared to respond. And we do not need Saddam Hussein to give us that wake-up call." [25] Senator Sam Nunn, chair of the Senate Armed Services Committee, put it this way:

> We do not have any carrier based anywhere near that country now. So if the president were to decide on some kind of military option, he would have to rely on what? He would have to rely primarily on long-range bombers, not with nuclear weapons, of course, but with conventional weapons.[26]

Senator John McCain advocated funds for construction of naval vessels, saying, "I do not have to make the case for the battleships. Saddam Hussein has made the case for the battleships." [27]

U.S. Middle East Policy: The Essential Continuities

The debate over the military at the close of the Cold War echoes the debate at the end of the Second World War. Those who called for limits on the U.S. military were overruled by the advocates of far-reaching military commitments—just as today, those who emphasize domestic economic and social concerns have been overridden by those who stress a continuing military superpower role in the post-Cold War period.

The U.S. mission was then termed "containment" of the Soviet Union, a strategic doctrine which held for nearly half a century. The formation of NATO in 1949 embodied the commitment of the United States to bipolarity and to "forward deployment" of U.S. troops.

The Middle East held an essential place in the concept of containment; with its connotation of defense, of containing Soviet aggression, the United States, paradoxically, projected its economic, political and military power into the region. With similar rhetoric today, Bush states that Iraqi "aggression cannot be rewarded" to justify a massive projection of U.S. military force into the Gulf. The extension of the policy of containment from Europe to the third world began in the Middle East in 1946. Most presidents since have given their names to doctrines of containment, either specifically directed towards or heavily affecting the Middle East and North Africa.

Until the Second World War, the United States was only a minor actor in the Middle East. The abrupt shift in the balance of power between western Europe and the United States during World War II broke that pattern, however. The economic, political and military power of the United States expanded in the region, as exhausted European colonial power contracted. The quest for geopolitical containment of the Soviet Union and the eagerness of U.S. corporations to exploit the oil in the area were knitted together tightly.

The Cold War in the third world was born in the northern province of Iran, which was occupied by Soviet troops during World War II while U.S. and British troops occupied the south. It is reported that President Truman resorted to nuclear threats to oust Soviet troops from northern Iran, a grim measure of the extent to which the U.S. government was committed to containing or even "rolling back" the Soviet Union in the region. With the Soviet withdrawal came the collapse of the Kurdish and Azerbaijani autonomous republics, established in 1945. In 1948, the United States granted $60 million in aid to the government of the Shah of Iran.

The Truman Doctrine

Early in 1947, Truman called for, and Congress granted, funds for aid to Greece and to its neighbor Turkey—"to support," as Truman put it, "free people who are resisting attempted subjugation by armed minorities or outside pressure." It would be an "unspeakable tragedy," he said, if these countries fell under Soviet domination, for then all of the Middle East might be "lost." This policy was known as the Truman doctrine.

A clandestine operation, part of this "Northern Tier" prioritization, was undertaken by the Central Intelligence Agency against the democratically elected government of Iran, which had nationalized the country's oil. A CIA-assisted coup toppled the government and restored the Shah to power. In a striking example of the interplay of economic interest, commercial rivalry and power projection, the nationalization of Iranian oil was reversed following the coup. When the corporate shares were reallocated, British ownership was reduced, replaced by the United States.

With the line drawn to the north, the United States turned its efforts toward aligning the states in the region with the United States and Western Europe, through the Baghdad Pact, conceived as an application of NATO to the Middle East/North Africa region.

The Eisenhower Doctrine

The Eisenhower doctrine extended the concept of containment from the Northern Tier to the entire region, grouping, under one ideological umbrella, Soviet troops and Arab nationalism. Under the Baghdad Pact, key states in the region would be linked to the West in alliance against the USSR and any progressive regional forces. Baghdad was an apt home for the pro-Western pact, since Iraq was still ruled by a Hashemite monarchy under very strong British influence.

With the departure of the colonial powers, there was a moment of euphoric hope in the region that a unified Arab state might finally emerge. But these hopes for unity had no place in the Eisenhower administration's view: regional aspirations were less significant than global superpower rivalries.

The initial Eisenhower doctrine target was Egypt's Gamal Abdul Nasser, who had angered the U.S. government by declining to affiliate with the Baghdad Pact and who had accepted weapons sales and development assistance from socialist countries after these were denied by the United States and Britain. In January 1957, Eisenhower declared that the United States is "prepared to use armed force" anywhere in the Middle East to counter "aggression from any country controlled by international communism." The idea that Nasser's Egypt was under such control was absurd: Egyptian communists faced repression and the composition and program of the Egyptian government were in no way communist.

The Eisenhower doctrine was invoked to project power into the region, under the guise of protecting states from Egyptian "aggression." In neither case were any Egyptian weapons, troops or personnel of any sort in or near the territory in question. U.S. troops intervened in the Lebanese civil war in 1958, a war which counterpoised a Maronite elite, which had been bequeathed substantial continuing political advantages by the departed French colonial order, against a combination of the elites of the Muslim communities and of the growing nationalist progressive movement. The real target of the U.S. Marines was even farther away from Egyptian "aggression," and was an ineffectual attempt to affect events in Iraq, where a British-imposed monarchy had just been toppled by a progressive nationalist movement. Iraqi adherence to the Baghdad Pact in the last years of the monarchy was one of the issues which provoked the revolution.

Jordan was also subjected to U.S. power. A new government had been freely elected, then an anomaly in Jordanian politics. This nationalist government opposed the Baghdad Pact, despite urging from the United States, and adopted instead positions which could be described generally as nonaligned and progressive. King Hussein

carried out a military coup against the elected government, British paratroopers arrived, and the United States
government announced a $10 million aid package to the
King under the Eisenhower doctrine.

The Kennedy and Johnson Policy

The Eisenhower doctrine had failed to persuade
most countries in the region to join a pro-western alliance
and had not stopped the spread of nationalism. Despite
fleeting explorations of a *rapprochement* with Nasser,
accommodation to Arab nationalism and establishment of
a *modus vivendi* with non-alignment under Kennedy, U.S.
antipathy to these phenomena was rapidly reasserted.

In 1967, the United States vehemently denounced
"Soviet clients" in the region—especially Egypt under
Nasser and Syria under the radical nationalist neo-Ba'ath
Party. The Johnson administration, already involved in a
losing war in Indochina, was in no position to muster
domestic political support for any U.S. intervention in the
Middle East and North Africa. In June 1967, Israel won
a stunning military and political victory over these two
putative "Soviet clients," along with the conquest of the
West Bank from King Hussein. The victory must have
seemed to strategists in Washington to be a perfect application in the Middle East of the concept which under-
pinned   President   Johnson's   Vietnamization
program—that regional forces should be bearing the
brunt of the battle against those which the United States
opposed.

The Nixon Doctrine

Following the Israeli victory in the 1967 War, the
United States began to give Israel significant military aid.
Coupled with the approach taken by the next administra-
tion—an approach which came to be known as the Nixon

doctrine—this represented a still further extension of the strategy of containment in the Middle East. In addition to aiding regimes along the Soviet periphery against insurgencies deemed to be emanating from the Soviet Union (as it had done under the Truman doctrine), the United States would pour military aid—and in some instances military training and technical advice—into countries to build armies which could maintain or impose on third countries the kind of order the United States wanted to see in the region. This would relieve the United States of the need to intervene directly against the Arab nationalist movement, as it had done under the Eisenhower doctrine.

Israel soon began to receive more U.S. security assistance than any other country in the world, still true to the present day. Between 1977 and 1989, Israel received $46 billion in U.S. aid, about a quarter of all U.S. foreign military and economic assistance.[28] Enormous amounts of economic assistance subsidized continued occupation of the West Bank and Gaza Strip. Although the aid was actively solicited by the Labor Alignment, which dominated every Israeli goverment from 1948 to 1976, the social and political impact probably fostered the growth of the Israeli right. By subsidizing settlements, the aid provided hothouse conditions for the rise of extremists, and by minimizing the economic impact of occupation on Israelis, it reduced any "braking" effect the economic costs might have had. In 1976, the right-wing Likud won the elections, and has been a factor in all Israeli governments since.

On the diplomatic front the United States has provided political support for the Israeli occupation, defying the international consensus—as reflected in resolutions of the United Nations General Assembly, the European Community and the Non-Aligned States—that an international conference should be convened to seek a peaceful resolution with an independent Palestinian state alongside Israel.

The Nixon Doctrine in the Gulf

In 1972, the United States sold advanced weaponry to the Shah of Iran, ostensibly to aid him in confronting his Soviet-armed neighbor, Iraq, and to exercise control in the crucial Gulf area after Britain withdrew from an exercise of power it could no longer afford. During the 1970s, the Shah contracted to buy $24 billion in weapons from the United States, a welcome new market for U.S. military contractors as the Vietnam War wound down. A shining exemplar of a Nixon doctrine client, the Shah dispatched troops to suppress an insurgency in the Dhofar province of Oman.

Under Nixon, the political, social, and economic lives of the recipient nations underwent substantial transformation. The engorgement of the military sector in Iran during the 1970s, for example, was so massive that it is considered a major factor in precipitating the revolution at the end of the decade. The Nixon doctrine collapsed with the fall of the Shah, and the entry of Soviet troops into Afghanistan signalled preparations for the direct dispatch of U.S. troops in the Gulf.

The Carter Doctrine: Focus on the Gulf

The Iranian regime provided a new challenge to the U.S. government, one which foreshadowed the problems of the post-Cold War period. Previous targets of U.S. wrath in the region had been depicted as somehow linked to the Soviet Union—if not actually communist, then clients of the Soviet Union, or proxies or recipients of Soviet weaponry. Though these characterizations often may have been misleading, they were consistent. But the Islamic Republic in Iran did not fit the mold: it was hostile to the Soviet Union, making it an implausible candidate for denunciation as a minion of the Kremlin. Even for purposes of domestic propaganda, the hoary charges of communism were useless: Americans had been taught that communists were godless, an accusation to which the Ayatollah was hardly vulnerable.

In January 1980, the Carter doctrine was outlined:

an attempt by any outside force to gain control of the Persian Gulf region will be regarded as an assault on the vital interests of the United States of America, and such an assault will be repelled by any means necessary, including military force.[29]

The Carter administration had turned toward a direct interventionist posture prior to that announcement. Strategic planning had vacillated between those arguing for a concentration of forces in Europe with a sharp decline in troop strength and limited prospects for U.S. military adventure abroad on the one hand, and those such as Samuel Huntington of Harvard on the other hand, who suggested that the Gulf, not the NATO region, was to become a prime arena of U.S.-Soviet confrontation.

Carter's national security adviser, Zbigniew Brzezinski, responded by refurbishing the old concept of a "fire brigade," a military unit especially equipped for quick response to "brushfire war" in the third world, calling it the Rapid Deployment Force, inaugurated in 1977. This marked a turning point in U.S. strategy: the naval presence which operated in the Gulf since the Second World War was expanded, and serious consideration of landing ground troops in the Gulf was incorporated for the first time.

The Reagan Doctrine

With the advent of Reagan came preparations for direct military intervention in the Gulf, against a backdrop of the intense militarization of the Middle East/North Africa region extending from Pakistan to Morocco. One index of this military concentration was the heavy proportion of U.S. security assistance which was earmarked for countries in the region.[30]

Reagan initiated the largest "covert" assistance program since the Vietnam War era through a campaign of aid to the Afghan Mujahadeen, which reached $660 million in fiscal year 1987.[31] While the administration's support for the Nicaraguan contras was opposed (albeit with varying degrees of success), the aid for their Afghan counterparts went virtually unchallenged, except by some Congresspeople who wanted to increase aid.

Reagan breached the barrier against the use of direct military force in the region which has been in place since the intensification of Arab nationalism in the 1960s and the domestic political opposition to foreign intervention brought on by the war in Indochina. U.S. Marines were deployed in Lebanon in 1983, under the guise of protecting the Palestinian civilian population after the withdrawal of PLO fighters from Beirut. But the U.S. military took on a role in the Lebanese civil war, putting its firepower at the disposal of the Lebanese government, which was receiving over $1 billion in military assistance from the United States. The U.S. incursion in Lebanon ended in disaster: a truck bomber crashed into the Marine barracks, killing 242 people. The force withdrew, lobbing huge shells at Lebanese villages from the Sixth Fleet offshore.

Under the Reagan administration, the U.S. Air Force bombed Libya in 1986, purportedly in retaliation for assistance policymakers believed Col. Muammar Qadafi had rendered to terrorists who bombed a nightclub frequented by U.S. soldiers. The bombing killed some 100 Libyans, principally civilians, among them the adopted infant daughter of Col. Qadafi.

Planning for a U.S. Base in Saudi Arabia

The United States undertook an ambitious and ex-

pensive base-building program to support its future operations in the region: during the 1980s, the United States
projected an expenditure of more than $14 billion dollars
to construct or expand a long chain of bases for its forces.[32]
Half a billion dollars was expended on Diego Garcia, little
more than a rock outcropping in the Indian Ocean, leased
from Britain and transformed into an air base to accommodate B-52s and a naval base for U.S. "prepositioned"
supply ships and other vessels. More than $270 million
was spent to build air and naval bases in Oman, a small
Gulf state, and a smaller amount in Bahrain. Other important facilities for Gulf operations were upgraded in
Morocco, Kenya, Somalia and Portugal, new agreements
were signed and pre-existing ones were maintained for
the use of facilities in Liberia, Djibouti, and the Sey-
chelles. The United States had tacit agreements for use of
air bases in Egypt (from which AWACs, for example, have
operated), Turkey (three NATO bases), and Saudi Arabia.[33]

     Saudi Arabia—until August 1990—had been unable
to accept a direct U.S. military presence in the kingdom.
Such a presence would render it vulnerable to critics who
decry assisting the major supporter of Israel, and would
entail cultural and religious difficulties. The United
States has over the years had informal access to Saudi
bases, and the facilities were "overbuilt" beyond Saudi
needs with an eye to possible future use by U.S. personnel.
Most of the Saudi military construction has been planned
and supervised by the U.S. Army Corps of Engineers.
Between 1950 and 1985, Saudi Arabia contracted for more
than $20.5 billion in military construction from the United
States.[34] Saudi Arabia has been the biggest market in the
world for U.S. exports of military equipment and services:
between fiscal years 1974 and 1987, for example, it bought
more than $51 billion in U.S. military exports.[35] In 1985,
some 6,190 U.S. civilian and military personnel were
stationed in Saudi Arabia to advise and support weapons

systems imported from the United States.[36] The training of the Saudi National Guard, for example, was contracted in large part to a U.S. corporation, Vinell.

In order to protect Saudi Arabia from a perceived threat from Iran, the United States sold Saudi Arabia five AWACs, aircraft designed both for surveillance and for command, communication and control functions. The AWACs could be fully integrated with a U.S. force deployed to the area in the future. The AWACs sale was part of an $8.2 billion arms deal to the Saudis, the single largest U.S. foreign arms deal. The package barely passed Congress after the opposition of the American Israel Public Affairs Committee and other supporters of the Israeli government. But fears that the weapons might be used against Israel were unrealistic. Their use was far more likely in a crisis such as the current one, given various provisions written into the agreement by the United States guaranteeing close U.S. control of the planes. The pattern of their deployment was clearly aimed at Iran. Nevertheless, Saudi efforts to purchase F-15s and Stinger missiles from the United States in 1985-86 failed; the Saudis then moved toward European arms suppliers.

The Reagan administration also transformed President Carter's Rapid Deployment Force into the Central Command, or USCENTCOM, which had the capacity to mobilize 320,000 troops from the Army, Navy and Marine Corps.

The United States and Iraq

As the United States continued its military buildup in Saudi Arabia and elsewhere in the Gulf region, its policy toward Iraq underwent a series of changes. The United States had a generally hostile relationship with Iraq after the monarchy was toppled in 1958. By the 1970s, close relations between Iraq and the Soviet Union had given that U.S. hostility a hard geopolitical edge.

During the 1970s, the Shah of Iran (who had a very adversarial relationship with the Ba'ath leadership of Iraq) was viewed as a friend of the United States confronting a Soviet client to his west. The Shah had been attempting to encourage another outbreak of rebellion by the Kurds of northern Iraq. The Kurds, a Muslim but not Arab people, had been denied their own independent Kurdistan when the victorious European Allies reneged on a wartime promise after World War I, and now live in parts of Turkey, Syria, Iraq and Iran. The Shah urged the Iraqi Kurds not to accept an autonomy plan offered to them by Baghdad after an insurgency, but to rise up in arms once again. The Kurdish leadership was reluctant to do so, and acted only on the assurance of the CIA that their effort would be assisted clandestinely by the United States. The CIA did indeed supply the Kurds with military equipment, but suddenly the U.S. position on relations between Iraq and Iran changed, and Henry Kissinger helped broker the Algiers Agreement resolving border disputes between Iraq and Iran. The CIA abruptly terminated its assistance to the Kurds leaving the insurgents—who in all probability would not have rebelled without the promises of the CIA—to be mopped up by the Iraqi regime. Kissinger responded to critics who deplored the cynical abandonment of the Kurds, by saying that clandestine operations are not "a mission activity." [37]

U.S. Policy and the Iran/Iraq War: Bleeding Both Sides

In 1980, Saddam Hussein thought he saw an opportunity for territorial aggrandizement in what he perceived as the disarray of the new Islamic Republic of Iran. Renouncing the Algiers Agreement, he reasserted claims to the disputed waterway of Shatt al Arab, and declared that he would free by military force the oppressed Arab population of Arabistan, who just happened to live in Iran's oil-rich Khuzistan province.

Washington took a benign view of his aggression against Iran, which was deemed a major threat to U.S. interests after the Shah's downfall. During eight years of war, Iraqi and Iranian casualties totalled between 500,000 and one million dead. The United States assisted both sides, but helped Iraq more. As a prerequisite to providing assistance, the U.S removed Iraq from its official list of "terrorist states." Agricultural import credits were furnished to Iraq, freeing up Iraqi hard currency for military imports; it was also given electronic intelligence data to assist it to target Iran.

At other points, the United States helped Iran, as in the notorious-arms-for-hostages deal and other projects which came to light in the Iran-Contra scandal. U.S. policy prolonged the war so that both countries might lose slowly. The Reagan administration originally called its policy "neutrality," a perverse statement. The depths of U.S. duplicity are illustrated by Operation Staunch, an effort to stop the flow of weapons to Iran, during which the United States allowed Israel to supply U.S.-manufactured spare parts to Iran.[38]

The theocratic tyranny of the Islamic Republic pitted against the brutal "Strongman of Iraq" made for a most improbable East/West conflict, given that both superpowers supplied weapons to each side at various points during the war and were primarily assisting Iraq by the end of the war. Nevertheless, President Reagan's National Security Paper maintained that it was a war which affected the regional balance between the superpowers:

> Iran's continuation and escalation of the Iran-Iraq war, including its attempts to intimidate nonbelligerent Gulf Arab states, pose the most serious, immediate threat to our interests, and provide the Soviet Union with the opportunity to advance its regional agenda.[39]

Reflagging Ships to Justify an Increased U.S. Presence

Under the cover of protecting commercial shipping, the United States increased its military presence in the Gulf through the reflagging operations of 1987-88. Measured against the stated objectives of protecting shipping, the operation was a failure: attacks on commercial shipping averaged eleven per month in the six months before the reflagging operation in July 1987 and rose to nineteen per month in the six months following the arrival of the huge U.S. armada. Caspar Weinberger's explanation of the operation as a "forward deployment of the U.S. navy" was more candid than others which described it as a defensive umbrella for commerce. By the end of the war, the United States was essentially functioning as an Iraqi military ally in the Gulf. In the process, the United States military had an opportunity to practice operations in the area which they would later use to attack Iraq.

U.S. Support for Iraq's Use of Chemical Weapons

The U.S. tacit alliance with Saddam Hussein survived his use of chemical weapons in his war with Iran, despite the horrible extent of the human damage wrought by Iraqi nerve and mustard gasses and other chemical weaponry: 600 Iranian "chemical casualties" by the end of 1983; 11,100 in 1986; 13,500 in 1987, and 13,300 in the first two and a half months of 1988, according to a "threat analyst" at the U.S Army Chemical School.[40] In March 1988, Saddam Hussein used chemical weapons against Iraqi citizens—Kurdish villagers in an area of northern Iraq that Iranian forces had briefly occupied, but had evacuated before the Iraqi military used its chemical arsenal. Thousands of villagers in Halabja and Dojaila were killed by mustard gas, and possibly by the nerve gases phosgene and cyanide.[41]

Throughout this period, and especially 1987-88, when Iraqi use of chemical weapons was more extensive, the U.S. government provided valuable assistance to Saddam Hussein, and indeed, by the end of this period was functioning as his tacit military ally. Recent administration statements, deploring the threat that Iraq's chemical weapons pose to U.S troops and Israeli civilians are thus somewhat ironic; only days before Iraq's invasion of Kuwait, the State Department was lobbying Congress to refrain from imposing sanctions on Iraq because of its chemical weapons use.[42]

Containment and the New World Order: Parallels and Differences

For 40 years, the United States conducted its relations with the Middle East under the strategic concept of "containment"—protecting the region from Soviet encroachment. Containment was a diction of defense justifying the reality of aggression. While claiming to fend off external intervention in the area, the United States was extending its economic, political and military control.

Now the old framework of the Cold War has collapsed. The Bush administration's New World Order includes U.S. military control of a resource-rich area upon which its allies and rivals, Japan and Europe, depend. The United States has deployed 430,000 troops to Arab territory at the invitation of the King of Saudi Arabia, whose regime has been reinforced by an elaborate network of U.S. military contractors, advisers and intelligence agents. Saddam Hussein has wrongly extended his military control over Kuwait; George Bush seems intent upon countering that wrong by extending still larger U.S. military control over the region.

In so doing, Bush is charting the post-Cold War
direction of the country away from investing in productive
infrastructure and social programs. Rather than competing with Japan and Europe over production, the United
States is honing its competitive edge by exerting military
control over the area which its rivals depend upon for oil.
The United States could engage its former superpower
rival in a joint venture to encourage negotiated resolution
of regional disputes. Instead, the Bush administration is
taking advantage of its erstwhile enemy's retirement from
the fray. With a new freedom from the fear of the Soviet
nuclear deterrent, it is intensifying the level of U.S military intervention in the Middle East.

While there are striking parallels between the initi-
ation of the containment and New World Order policies,
there are very important differences. Between the late
1940s and the mid-1950s, U.S. corporations dramatically
increased their equity interest in Middle Eastern oil,
acquisitions considerably assisted by the regional political
and military power of the United States. The economic
and political power of the United States was also in
concert in Europe and Japan; the economic policies of the
Marshall Plan fostered the conversion of Europe from a
coal-fueled to an oil-powered economy, and the purchase
of U.S. corporate "dollar oil" rather than British "sterling
oil" from the Middle East, and followed a similar pattern
through the Occupation Government of Japan.

Today, U.S.-based transnational corporations no
longer "own" Middle Eastern oil; in 1972, international oil
companies had an equity interest in 92 percent of the oil
leaving the Middle East, a figure which plummeted to
under 7 percent within ten years, as the producing countries took on a greater degree of control over their resources.[43] The energy corporations are still enormously
powerful, and garnered windfall profits during the first
six months of the U.S. deployment in the Gulf, as oil prices
shot up. But they do not have the economic control they

once had. Now, as U.S. economic power declines, military power grows.

The economic rivals of the United States, moreover, have increased their commercial role in the Gulf, while their military encumbrances remain minimal or nonexistent. Japan and the United States are about even in their civilian market shares in Saudi Arabia, for example, while Japan only bears the costs of voluntary "contribution" to the war.

These regional realities compound the general problem that the United States faces as a declining economic power whose president has chosen an expanding military role. The now tottering economy could stagger more severely; the social tensions which are bound to be generated by a war fought so disproportionately by minorities and working-class youth could tear major holes in an already tattered social fabric.

As General Colin Powell told the District of Columbia Bar Association shortly before the aerial bombardment began, "War is a terrible thing with unpredictable consequences." [44] It is a risky option that the Bush administration has chosen, one which seems designed to fail. What no one can know is how many people must die before this option is laid aside.

Notes

1. Transcript of a discussion between Iraqi President Saddam Hussein and Ambassador April Glaspie, July 25, 1990. This transcript was released by the government of Iraq. Its accuracy has not been challenged by the U.S. government.

2. Quoted in *Armed Forces Journal International*, September 1990, p. 5.

3. Theodore C. Sorenson, "Rethinking National Security," *Foreign Affairs*, Summer, 1990, Vol. 69, No. 3. p. 1.

4. Sorenson, *op. cit.*, p. 4.

5. Paul Kennedy, *The Rise and Fall of the Great Powers: Economic Change and Military Conflict from 1500 to 2000*, New York: Random House, 1987.

6. Kennedy, *op. cit.*, p. xvi.

7. William G. Hyland, "America's New Course," *Foreign Affairs*, Spring 1990, Vol. 69, No. 2, p. 3.

8. McNamara to committee.

9. Colin Gray, "Tomorrow's Forecast: Warmer/Still Cloudy," *Proceedings of the U.S. Naval Institute*, May, 1990. Vol. 116/5/1,047 p. 38.

10. Interview with Vice President Dan Quayle, *Armed Forces Journal International*, February 9, 1990, p. 70.

11. General Colin Powell, in testimony before the Senate Budget Committee, February 5, 1990, quoted in *Armed Forces Journal International*, March, 1990, p. 12.

12. General Colin Powell, "Crystal Balls Don't Always Help," Proceedings of the U.S. Naval Institute, May 1990, Vol. 116/5/1,047, p. 64.

13. General Carle E. Vuono, Chief of Staff, U.S. Army, in testimony before the U.S. Congress, House Armed Services Committee, *Department of Defense Authorization for Appropriation, FY 1990-1991, U.S. Military Posture and Budget Overview*, May 4, 1989, p. 137.

14. General A.M. Gray, Commandant, U.S. Marine Corps, "Defense Policy for the 1990s," *Marine Corps Gazette*, May 1990, Vol. 74, No. 5, p. 19.

15. *Ibid.*

16. Commission on Integrated Long-Term Strategy, *Discriminate Deterrence*, p. 2.

17. *Ibid.*, p. 13.

18. William W. Kaufmann and Lawrence J. Korb, "The 1990 Defense Budget," *Studies in Defense Policy*, Washington, D.C. 1989.

19. Congressperson Les Aspin, January 12, 1990.

20. Lt. General E. Mundy, Jr., *Navy Times*, January 1990.

21. Robert K. Ropelweski, "How Panama Worked, Planning, Precision and Surprise Lead to Panama Success," *Armed Forces Journal International*, February 1990, p. 26.

22. Interview with Caspar Weinberger, *Proceedings of the U.S. Naval Institute*, May 1990, Vol. 116/5/1,047. p. 49.

23. Michel McQueen, *Wall Street Journal*, January 19, 1990.

24. Carol Matlack, *National Journal*, April 14, 1990.

25. *Bulletin of the Atomic Scientist*, "Bulletin," vol 46 No. 7, Sept 1990, p. 11.

26. *Ibid.*

27. *Ibid.*

28. *Background Materials on Foreign Assistance*, Report of the Task Force on Foreign Assistance to the Committee on Foreign Affairs, U.S. House of Representatives, February 1989. p. 160.

29. President Jimmy Carter, State of the Union Address, January 1980.

30. *Background Materials on Foreign Assistance, op. cit.*

31. *Washington Post.*

32. Martha Winger, Joe Stork, and Dick Anderson, "Living by the Sword in the Middle East: A Primer," *Middle East Report*, Januaury/February 1987, Vol. 17, No. 1, p. 24.

33. Anthony Cordesman, *The Gulf and the West: Strategic Relations and Military Realities*, Boulder: Westview Press, 1988.

34. Cordesman, *op. cit.*, pp. 194-197.

35. Cordesman, *op. cit.*, p. 196.

36. Cordesman, *op. cit.*, pp. 204-205.

37. See Henry Kissinger, *Years of Upheaval,* Boston: Little Brown, 1982.

38. These events were recounted in the Pike Report, leaked in part to the press, but never published in full. See an excellent piece by Christopher Hitchens, *Harpers,* January 1991.

39. "National Security of the United States," White House, 1988.

40. Lee Waters, "By the Poisons of Babylon," *Defense and Diplomacy,* January/February 1991, Vol. 9, No. 1-2.

41. Cordesman, op. cit p. 431.

42. Speech of Senator Daniel Moynihan on the Senate floor, January 11, 1991.

43. "Middle East Oil: An Uncertain Future," *The Middle East* (7th edition), Washington, D.C.: Congressional Quarterly, 1990, p. 112.

44. *Washington Post,* January 12, 1991.

War Over Access to Cheap Oil, or the Reassertion of U.S. Hegemony?

Debunking a Popular Myth

Cyrus Bina

To say that oil figures prominently in the Persian Gulf crisis is to state the obvious. But what exactly is its role? Winston Churchill once noted that the prize in the Middle East is not the use of oil but the mastery of oil. Cyrus Bina has been analyzing the economic forces driving the global oil industry for many years, and here lays bare the history of the mechanisms that control price rises and drops. He delivers a compelling argument that the United States is attempting to maintain its mastery over the distribution and pricing of oil, not its access to the resource.

The United States is not in the Persian Gulf to protect access to cheap oil. Many people opposed to U.S. policy believe that the wasteful use of oil has led us to use military might in service of a lifestyle built on cheap oil. In support of this view, political cartoons admonish our desire to fight for the protection of the right to drive at 18 miles to the gallon. Many have pointed to the spectacle of Bush riding his boat that guzzles 25 gallons an hour as a symbol of our disregard for conservation and evidence that Bush seeks to protect a bad lifestyle choice. Indeed, Bush has mentioned the need for Americans to conserve

71

exactly once since the crisis began, and only at the prompt-
ing of reporters. But defense of the right to waste energy
is not what is driving U.S. policy.

To understand what role oil plays in U.S. policy in
the Persian Gulf crisis, there are some useful parallels
with the oil crisis of 1973-74. In each case, any shortage
was relatively short-lived. In the current crisis, missing
production from Kuwait and Iraq has been supplied by
other oil-producing nations. A real long-term oil shortage
may well be centuries away. Current reserves include one
trillion barrels of oil—forty years' supply at current rates.
Further development of oil and related products could
produce an estimated 3.4 trillion barrels. But the lack of
any shortage should not mitigate concern for the ecology.
As *The Left Business Observer* points out,

> ...the earth could become uninhabitable in the process of
> developing, refining, and burning these liquid fossils. A
> physical shortage of breathable air and drinkable water
> is much closer; that should be the real motive force behind
> an energy policy—not narcissistic nightmares of depen-
> dence or Malthusian ones of fuel famine.[1]

In addition to an absence of a long-term shortage in
either crisis, in both situations preserving access to cheap
oil was not the fundamental motivation of U.S. capitalism.

Predominant Theories
about the Control of Oil

The major theories explaining how oil is priced
would suggest that it is in U.S. interests to keep oil as
inexpensive as possible. But in reviewing the history of oil
development, it becomes clear that it is the control of oil
and its role in the global economy that motivates U.S.
policy, not ensuring a continued, inexpensive supply for
the United States. Theories of what governs the flow and
price of oil generally fall into three categories: traditional,

dependency, and conspiracy theories. Their use and limits can best be seen by applying them to the crisis of 1973-74 when prices nearly quadrupled.

Traditional theories of the 1973-74 oil crisis incorporate several arguments. Raymond Vernon, among others, argued that an imbalance in "supply and demand" led to the crisis—demand outstripped supply and the price rose until demand slackened.[2] Others argued that the Organization of Petroleum Exporting Countries (OPEC) operated as a monopoly, able to raise prices at will.[3] The dependence of the United States on foreign oil is also cited as a determining factor.[4] John Blair argued that the crisis might have been avoided had the suddenness of the price increase occurred over a longer time period.[5] While those espousing the traditional theory of the crisis placed different emphasis on these factors, they all agreed that it was the actors in the crisis who decided to raise the price of oil. None realized the structural changes in the development of oil in the United States and the internationalization of the oil industry that made the price increase inevitable; the former continues to govern oil production today.

A closer look reveals that while there was a shortage of oil during the crisis, it was limited and soon overcome. Yet prices did not fall after the end of the shortage. This fact calls into question the validity of the "supply and demand" theory; as supply grew after the shortage, prices should have fallen. Further, during the recession of 1974-75, demand slackened considerably, which in turn should have caused the prices to drop. But substantially higher price levels were maintained both after the shortage and still later after demand fell.

Traditional theorists counter that OPEC, acting as a monopoly, was able to hold the price of oil regardless of demand and supply fluctuations. Further, U.S. "dependence" on foreign oil exacerbated the crisis.[6] But while these observations of OPEC's power at the time and U.S. dependence on foreign oil are correct, the conjunction of these facts fails to build an explanation of the dynamics behind the crisis.

The second group of theories, the dependency theories, argue that OPEC was able to launch a "price offensive" because of the political changes of the time. Namely, it was a reaction to the long domination of the third world by the industrial nations. This essentially political argument is mixed into the economic argument which emphasizes monopoly power.

Yes, there was monopoly in the oil industry, but that should not be confused with a lack of competition. As Marx put it, "*competition* is nothing other than the *inner nature of capital;* [here] its essential character, appearing in and realized as the reciprocal interaction of many capitals with one another, [that is] the inner tendency as external necessity." [7] This process of competition grows more intense, not less intense, as capital accumulates. As John Weeks notes, "It is with the development of capital in its most advanced form, monopoly capital, that competition, too, develops to its fullest extent." [8] It is a mistake to equate competition with a large number of firms in an industry, and lack of competition with few firms. Monopoly and competition cannot be dichotomized based upon the number of firms in an industry. In fact, oil markets are quite competitive today. A further feature often cited to argue that the industry is uncompetitive is the size of the big oil companies. Yet size must not be confused with profitability. Contrary to popular wisdom, this big industry is not as profitable as many other businesses.

While the facts marshalled in the service of dependency theory—the United States' political decline in the post-Vietnam War era, and OPEC's increased income—are compelling, they do not in themselves explain the nature of the oil crisis.

The third set of theories are based on ideas of conspiracy: with the rivalry between Japan, Europe, and the United States intensifying, a conspiracy to raise the price

of oil would harm those economies competing with the
United States more than it would the U.S. economy. While
this rivalry is deeper today, the theory was also applied
to the crisis of 1973-74. Even though the United States
became a major importer during the early 1970s, it is
argued, correctly, that the price burden fell more heavily
on Japan and Europe.[9] But, as with the other theories,
observation of the facts does not constitute a theory. The
relatively more severe impact on those economies relying
more heavily on oil imports does not have anything to do
with the causes of the change in the price of oil, unless it
is true that the price of oil is determined by the U.S.
government, by oil companies, or by OPEC's discretion.
There is little evidence to support this theory, and above
all it is impossible to verify. The lack of validity is due, as
will be shown below, to mistaking the facts for the essential reasons why the crisis came into being.

An Alternative Analysis

Despite the oil crisis of 1973-74 being triggered by a
war, the resulting huge price increases were due to take
place in any case as a consequence of the significant
long-term increase in production costs of oil in the United
States prior to October 1973. The least productive of the
oil regions in the world is the United States. For many
years, production in this country has also been the most
expensive in the world.[10] As will be demonstrated below,
it was the retention of aged U.S. oil fields, which resulted
in decline in the average oil recovery, that was the underlying factor necessitating the reorganization of production, the change in market price, and new royalties in the
international petroleum industry.

If old oil fields in the United States necessitated the
rise in prices to recoup production costs, several questions
must be answered: Why weren't those fields abandoned in
favor of more productive ones? If the industry is a compet-

itive one, why didn't the more expensive fields simply get phased out in favor of more productive and cheaper fields?

Expensive, old fields continue to be used primarily because development of new discoveries was unfeasible in the United States. Although there are more productive fields that could be developed, the pattern of capitalist land ownership discourages this. Since an oil field lies under land usually owned by many different parties, development of a field is complicated. Obtaining the rights to drill on one person's land does not prevent competition for the same field by other companies, who can start up through leasing someone else's land over the same field. In addition, to get the largest feasible quantity of oil from a field, the drilling of wells must be coordinated for that extraction. At the same time, for the secondary recovery, the entire oil field must be under the control of one management. Haphazard drilling would prevent the realization of the potential of the field.

The result of these factors arising from the pattern of land ownership in the United States is that the full benefits of discovery of new fields will rarely go to the primary discoverer. In fact, "...the percentage of the benefits from a well received by the discoverer declines with the size of the field." [11]

For these reasons, it is more profitable to invest in already discovered and working fields than in new and theoretically cheaper finds. In turn, the increasing volume of capital investments in the existing oil fields, and the production of reserves by way of intensification, extension, and enhanced recovery methods, led to the subsequent decline of average oil recovery per well in the aging U.S. fields. The U.S. oil fields in the lower 48 states now constitute the least productive region in the world. [12]

By contrast, OPEC countries could rent out the rights to drill under their land in such a manner as to circumvent the impediments imposed on exploration and development in the United States by the distribution of land rights.

Increase in the international price followed lockstep from the increase in production costs in the United States, given the globalization of the industry that brought about unified pricing. During 1971-74, U.S. capital expenditure per barrel tripled. This increase mirrored the tripled level of U.S. oil prices during the same period. With the internationalization of oil production, the global price of oil was now determined by the newly-emerged U.S. cost structure.

Why didn't the United States let the aged fields fall out of production in favor of prices being set by more productive and cheaper fields in other countries? And why didn't the international market squeeze out these fields because of their unproductive nature?

To answer these questions, it is important to realize the size of the industry in the United States. In 1973-74, the United States was still the largest nation among oil-producing countries. Today, it is second only to the USSR. This fact alone made it unlikely that the plug would be pulled. Secondly, if the most unproductive fields were to be eliminated, the bulk of U.S. oil production originating from the more productive areas would have to remain intact. Other, relatively less productive fields located in the North Sea and elsewhere, along with the least productive U.S. fields, would be squeezed out of the market before the entire production from the United States.

Further, by allowing the price structure to be emerged in conjunction with the general rate of profit associated with the most expensive fields, other more productive oil regions could reap super profits over and above the general rate of the industry in the form of oil rents. The interests of OPEC, who could produce oil more cheaply than the United States, lay not in undercutting U.S. production through cheaper pricing. Rather, their interests lay in a price structure based on the higher costs of production in the United States, allowing them to be very profitable. Likewise, ironically, an increase in the

U.S. oil imports from OPEC and other productive regions of the world (given the demand) is an indication of forcing the least productive domestic oil fields out of business. This may, in turn, lead to a lower cost structure for the entire global oil industry.

Thus the OPEC "price offensive" in 1973-74 was not due to U.S. dependence on foreign oil. Nor was it due to diminished U.S. power. Rather, it was required in order to support the costs of continuing production in aged U.S. fields. In summary, three factors contributed to the price rise. First is the internationalization of the petroleum industry and *unification* of all the existing oil-producing regions of the world since the early 1970s. Second is the recognition of the characteristic of specific property relations (such as mineral rights and lease ownership) that are associated with the production of oil, and that are conceptually functioning as the foundation of oil royalties and rents. Finally, one has to recognize the effect of the intensification of capital investments within the least productive oil regions (such as the U.S. region) that, together with the above conditions, set the stage for the determination of higher production prices for the entire oil industry from the early 1970s onward. In other words, OPEC did what it did because the entire oil industry was at the threshold of a *social transformation* that practically revolutionized its institutional structure, and not the other way around.

The Gulf Crisis and Oil

As we have seen, the United States is not in the Persian Gulf to protect access to cheap oil. This is corroborated by a mission Bush undertook as vice president following the price declines in 1986 resulting from overproduction and the subsequent world oil glut. Bush's task was to stop the fall of oil prices, preventing the economic demise in the southern oil-producing states.

It is easy to cast Bush's trip in the light of self-interest as an oil man from Texas. But this analysis is short-sighted. As the executive coordinator of ruling-class interests, it is important that Bush help the ailing economy in the South not in the interests of oil companies, but in the interests of averting or limiting recession. Allowing prices to fall still further would have had an impact on the South in the same way that shutting down all the auto factories would have in Detroit.

It may be tempting to conclude, from the foregoing analysis of the 1973-74 oil crisis, that the current Gulf crisis is being used to raise the price of oil to a new level that is in conformity independent of the crisis with additional capital investment in the existing oil fields in the United States. This is incorrect.

While prices have risen dramatically because of the Gulf crisis, they have fluctuated wildly as a result of political instability and over speculation that a diplomatic solution might be found. Following the commencement of U.S. bombing of Iraq and Kuwait, prices dropped by over $10 a barrel in the optimistic belief that the conflict might be short. (These fluctuations have been less apparent at the pump due to outright price-gouging and as a result of a five-cent per gallon tax to reduce the federal deficit enacted in December 1990.) This indicates that the price changes are not a result of new requirements resulting from the restructuring of the oil industry, but rather a purely speculative reaction to the crisis itself. Indeed, this analysis is reinforced by the situation of semi-glut prior to Iraq's invasion of Kuwait.

Bush has declared that this conflict is not over oil. But while it is not over the oil in Kuwait or in Iraq directly, the conflict stems from the decline of U.S. global hegemony and the U.S. government's reaction to prevent it. To the extent that oil has been the *sine qua non* of this hegemony, it has something to do with oil. As a result, the current crisis cannot be explained as a fight over access to oil alone. Thus, any threat to the status quo, including Saddam's attempts to revive the spirit of pan-Arabism *vis-a-vis* the industrialized nations of the West headed by the United States, must be vigorously countered in the interests of the global capitalist order.

U.S. efforts to maintain its hegemony over the region, and much of the third world, are undergoing dramatic changes. At the peak of its global hegemony, the United States, via the Nixon doctrine, promised to control the third world through its designated local representatives. Israel has been the main base and springboard for U.S. interests and represents the incorporation of an external force in the region. The task of policing the region in the Persian Gulf fell to the Shah of Iran, who was also a source of inspiration for other client states including Saudi Arabia, Kuwait, and other reactionary regimes in the region. But in the present era of hegemonic decline (and the loss of its best puppets), the United States seems to have no choice except to replicate the activities of its early postwar years by going undisguised. Here, where the early naked aggressions were once the reflection of U.S. ascendance, its present aggressions (especially the U.S. actions in the Persian Gulf) are the signs of a reaction to its decline.

Notes

1. Henwood, Doug, *The Left Business Observer*, 40, 4 September 1990.

2. Vernon, Raymond, "An Interpretation," *Daedalus*, CIV, 4, Fall 1975, 1-14.

3. Penrose, Edith, "The Development of the Crisis," *Daedalus* CIV, 4, Fall 1975, 39-57.

4. McKie, James, "The United States," *Daedalus* CIV, 4, Fall 1975, 73-90, and Blair, John, *The Control of Oil*, New York: Pantheon, 1976.

5. *Ibid*, Blair.

6. Dasgupta, P.S., & Heal, G.M., *Economic Theory and Exhaustible Resources*, Cambridge: Cambridge University Press.

7. Marx, Karl, *Grundrisse*, New York: Vintage Books, 1973, 414, emphasis in original.

8. Weeks, John, *Capital and Exploitation*, Princeton: Princeton University Press, 1981, p. 167.

9. Greider, W. & Smith, J.P., "A Proposition: High Oil Prices Benefit U.S.," *The Washington Post*, July 10, 1977, p. A1.

10. Wyant, Frank, R., *The United States, OPEC, and Multinational Oil*, Lexington, MA: D.C. Heath, 1979.

11. Miller, E., "Some Implications of Land Ownership Patterns for Petroleum Policy," *Land Economics* 1973, 49(4).

12. Bina, Cyrus, *The Economics of the Oil Crisis*, London: The Merlin Press; New York: St. Martin's Press, 1985.

The Quest for Empire and the Struggle for Peace and Justice

Manning Marable

What are the domestic realities of an empire that rules by the sword? Marable makes clear the link between the costs incurred at home and those who suffer directly at the hands of an empire's military adventures. He locates the defining feature of the "American century" in the quest for empire. In his State of the Union Address, President Bush promised a second such century. But there is cause for hope. In sounding the call for resistance, noting that protest is the only language political elites are capable of understanding, Marable draws on an historical lesson from the Pentagon Papers: *domestic dissent is key to ending war.*

Every empire requires an external enemy in order to justify its measures to suppress domestic unrest and to silence its internal critics. Every empire must have a focal point to channel its aggressive objectives. Ancient Rome had Carthage; Napoleon had the British. The fundamental basis of the "American century" has been the quest for empire. In Southeast Asia, the declared goal of "containing communism" was responsible for the deaths of 50,000 American troops and millions of additional casualties among the Vietnamese people. The propaganda of American power has always created external enemies, larger-than-life figures which are used to justify massive military expenditures.

Saddam Hussein is only the latest in a series of "political demons" created by the U.S media, government officials and corporate elite. In an infantile language more appropriate to Saturday afternoon wrestling matches on television, the public villification of Saddam is personalized by Bush and his flunkies to preserve corporate domination of world oil markets, to assert American military hegemony in the Mideast, to fill the vacuum left by the Soviets, and to manipulate the masses of U.S. citizens into endorsing a war in which thousands of innocent people are victims.

In the euphoria generated by America's blitzkrieg against Iraq in the opening days of the war, the stock market soared and oil prices fell dramatically. The American people were told that the fruits of war would be the easy destruction of an evil dictator, the crushing of international terrorism and the reestablishment of the U.S. as a superpower.

Few measured the real human costs of war, upon both its victors and victims. The fruits of war are young children who must be told that their father, a young flight lieutenant, was shot down in his F-16 fighter over Baghdad never to return home. The fruits of war are the mothers and fathers of wounded and captured soldiers, who must worry as only parents can about their children, and yet are powerless to do anything about it. The fruits of war are young women and men who will lose their limbs, or will be paralyzed or blinded by mortar fire, and must be retrained to enter the workforce. The fruits of war are the thousands of American families whose economic lives are disrupted, pushed to the edge of bankruptcy, fallen behind in mortgage payments, because one parent in the army reserve has been shipped out to Saudi Arabia.

Then there are the fruits of war for Iraqis and Kuwaitis. Television reporters tell us about "surgical air strikes" by American bombers, a concept both absurd and dishonest. Pilots speeding at one thousand miles per hour,

dropping one-ton bombs guided by lasers, are not conducting kidney transplants or brain microsurgery. They are
obliterating families, homes, mosques, and centers of
daily life. The sixteen-year-old boys in the Iraqi army are
not the security thugs who raped and murdered Kuwaiti
people. They are also the innocent victims, sacrificing
their lives beneath American bombardments.

This unnecessary, avoidable and indefensible war is
not against Saddam Hussein. It is, in effect, a massive
attack against the Iraqi people specifically, and generally
against the entire Arab world. The fruits of war are guilt,
shame, and moral irresponsibility for acts of military
terrorism which equal or exceed those committed in Kuwait by Saddam Hussein.

Redefining American Democracy

The demise of the Cold War and the defeat of Communism created a wave of political euphoria and self-con-
gratulation which was eclipsed only by the recent conflict
in the Persian Gulf. Political and corporate leaders, ideo-
logues and media pundits alike used the collapse of the
Berlin Wall as a metaphor for the failure of socialism and
the greatness of America's capitalist system. How lucky
we are, we were told, to live in such a free and wonderful
country!

But the rhetoric of democracy has never been more
than a bitter illusion for millions of Americans, trapped
in second-class status by race, gender, poverty, unemployment, and hunger. How democratic is this country, when
millions go to bed hungry each night? How do we justify
the fact that 30 percent of the American troops in Saudi
Arabia are African Americans, while the administration
which sent them vetoed the 1990 Civil Rights Act, and
attempted to outlaw minority scholarships to colleges?

People of color and other oppressed people must ask
themselves, what should constitute a constructive rela-

tionship between people and their government? Within a democracy, what do people have a right to expect, in terms of the conditions of daily life? What obligations does the government have to address patterns of institutional racism, sexism, and poverty? American capitalism is an economic system which is based on competition, and on the acquisition of wealth and property at the expense of others. It's a "zero sum game," like power, in which there are winners and losers. The political system reflects this winner-take-all logic, with politicians being marketed like grocery items. The wealthy elites control political outcomes through campaign contributions, financing incumbents. The media plays a supportive role in this process by pretending that the American electorate has real choices to select from between the candidates. We have competition without real choice in America.

Capitalism also fosters extreme individualism and materialistic values. The dynamics of the marketplace are replicated in daily human relations, as people are reinforced to perceive each other more as objects than as human beings. This is why our politicians are willing to leave thousands of homeless people to die in our streets each year, and millions more to remain trapped in the ghetto with inferior schools, substandard housing, and high joblessness.

To take but one example of life in the empire behind the curtain of democracy, inequality in our system is largely perpetuated by the health care system which is set up along profit-motive lines. Wealthy people in this country receive the best hospital care in the world. Yet millions of new jobs generated in the past decade do not have health benefits. We remain the only western, industrialized society in the world which lacks a comprehensive system of national health care. Thirty-seven million Americans have no medical or hospitalization insurance.

The human consequences of this anti-democratic health system are millions of premature deaths. A recent study in the *Journal of the American Medical Association* of nearly six hundred thousand Americans hospitalized in 1987 found that the death rate for uninsured patients was up to 3.2 times higher than for patients with health insurance. Uninsured patients were less likely to be given high-cost care, and more likely to have a shorter stay. Thousands of poor, unemployed, and blue collar working women and men will die needlessly. Millions of hours of productivity on the job are lost, and billions of dollars in potential tax revenues are lost as well.

Theoretically, we have a political democracy in this country, but we do not yet have an economic democracy, a system which provides basic guarantees for universal health care, housing, and full employment. To realize the dream of Martin Luther King, Jr., and other Americans who have sacrificed their lives to extend the principles of democracy to all, we must redefine the relationship between people and government, even as we work on the Persian Gulf crisis. Human needs, not competition and selfish individualism, must determine government policies, if democracy is to become a reality.

To return to the Persian Gulf crisis, the only positive fruits produced by war are the protests of those who oppose death and destruction. People of conscience are taking a stand. In Hiroshima, survivors of the 1945 atomic bombing staged a sit-in. In Germany, one hundred thousand marched the day after the war began. In San Francisco, nearly one thousand antiwar demonstrators were arrested, the most ever in a single day in that city's turbulent history. In New York City, five thousand protested, tying up traffic for hours. Major demonstrations were organized in Washington, D.C. The bitter fruits of war will only be ended when the American people regain control of their own government, demanding an end to the politics of empire and violence, which threatens the peace of the world.

The only language the American political and corpo-

rate elite understands is resistance. This means conducting teach-ins, explaining why the war is unnecessary. It
means civil disobedience, marches, demonstrations, and
political organizing, bringing together religious groups,
trade union, civil rights, feminist and other progressive
constituencies. Creative, democratic protest for peace
abroad and social justice at home should be our focus.

"Womenandchildren"

Propaganda Tools of Patriarchy

Cynthia Enloe

Does having women in the U.S. military advance the cause of feminism? How has their role in the Gulf crisis been portrayed in the United States and to what ends? In a comprehensive analysis, Enloe looks at the connections between women in the military, soldiers' conceptions of manliness, and the IMF strategies for handling third world debt.

In the torrents of media coverage that accompany an international crisis, women typically appear as symbols, victims, or dependents. "Womenandchildren" rolls so easily off network tongues because in network minds women are family members rather than independent actors, presumed to be almost childlike in their innocence about the *realpolitik* of international affairs. Rarely are women imagined to reveal any of the basic structures of a dangerous confrontation.

If there is an image that defines television's Gulf Crisis, it's a disheveled white woman coming off a 747, an exhausted baby on her shoulder. States exist, this media story implies, to protect womenandchildren. U.S. intervention in the Gulf would be harder to justify if there were no feminized victim. The real diplomatic wives, the British and American women who in the last decade have created formidable lobbying organizations to press for their interests, don't fit this scenario.

It follows that the Gulf Crisis story must also ignore

the female attaché at the American embassy in Kuwait, negotiating with the Iraqis for the release of these very same womenandchildren. Passing over women's organizing within the State Department, which opened up the previously masculinized foreign service, the media treats her merely as an honorary man: capable, able to take care of herself—and others. Her existence is not allowed to disturb the womenandchildren-protected-by-states'-men scenario.

To make sense of the Persian Gulf crisis, one has to listen to the different groups of women on whom the various governments are depending to help them implement their foreign policies. We are living in a world that is more understandable if we picture it as an artifice constructed out of unequal, fragile relationships between different groups of women and men. In the Persian Gulf this means not only European and American hostages, but also domestic servants, Arab feminists, women consumers and workers, diplomatic wives, military wives, and American women soldiers. It is taking considerable efforts by male officials to make each group of women play their conventional parts.

Though you don't see them on the evening news, there are an estimated 17,000 Filipino women working as domestic servants in Saudi Arabia. Thousands of others have been cleaning, washing, and minding children in Kuwait and the United Arab Emirates. Together, there are over 29,000 Filipino domestic servants in the Middle East. Government officials in many third world countries have been counting on the paychecks that maids send home to lessen their nations' imbalance of payments and to keep the lid on politically explosive unemployment.

These Asian women, now trapped in occupied Kuwait or crowded into Jordanian refugee camps, have been crucial players in reducing global tensions generated by international debt in the 1980s.

After the 1970s oil boom, Kuwaiti and Saudi women

became employers in their homes. But their relationships with their Sri Lankan or Filipino maids had to be devised in ways that met with their governments' and their husbands' approval, while keeping the foreign workers at least minimally content. As stories filtered back of the abuse that some—not all—Asian domestic servants experienced, the Sri Lankan and Philippine governments have been pressed by their own women's advocates to protect their nationals working abroad. These regimes have acted ineffectually, in part because they've been afraid of offending gulf states on whom they depend for oil, in part because they have concluded, they need to satisfy the men from the IMF, obsessed with balance of payments more than they need to win the support of their own domestic women's movements.

Caryle Murphy, The *Washington Post* reporter who sent out clandestine reports from Kuwait in the days following the Iraqi invasion, has described how some Filipino maids were taken by their Kuwaiti employers to the Philippine embassy for their safety. Other Kuwaitis, she reports, fled in front of the invading troops, leaving their maids to fend for themselves. Filipinas in Kuwait City told Murphy that they'd heard stories of Iraqi soldiers raping other domestic workers. Rape in war is never simply random violence. It is structured by male soldiers' notions of their masculine privilege, by the strength of the military's lines of command, and by class and ethnic inequalities among women. If you're a rich Kuwaiti woman you have less chance of being raped than if you are an Asian maid.

To make sense, then, of the Iraqi occupation of Kuwait, we have to talk about soldiers' ideas of manliness, middle-class women's presumptions about housework, and the IMF's strategies for handling international debt, all in the same breath. Debt, laundry, rape, and conquest are understandable only in relation to each other.

Though we have a hard time understanding it, to

Jordanians, Palestinians, and other Arabs, Saddam Hussein is a potent symbol of nationalist aspirations, which are fueled by a resentment of European and American attempts to impose their values and their priorities on the societies of the Middle East. To many Arab nationalist men, women are the people most vulnerable to Western coruption and exploitation. This passionate conviction has infused the political debates over women's attire and women's education.

But Middle East women are not mere symbols. First, they are diverse, distinguished by ethnicity, ideology, class, and nationality. Second, since the turn of the century many have been actively participated in their countries' freedom movements. Arab feminists have criticized many of their male compatriots for trying to fashion a nationalism that camouflages male privilege under the legitimizing cloak of "Arab tradition." While being a feminist nationalist in any community is a daunting project, being an Arab feminist nationalist is especially risky. In the Middle East, a woman's rights advocate is open to the double-barreled charge, leveled at her by nervous men, that she is succumbing to alien Western bourgeois values, while simultaneously splitting the nation at a time when it needs unity above all else.

The current Gulf crisis, defined largely by massive U.S. military posturing, has radically complicated local feminists' task. Arab women activists, walking a tightrope between male nationalists' patriarchy and Western policymakers' cultural imperialism, have the most to lose when an international crisis polarizes internal debate. Western male officials who claim that their policies are supporting "civilized" politics are, in fact, painting Arab women into an oppressive corner.

Yet, many observers are portraying wartime mobilization as good for women. Saddam Hussein, a secular, not a religious nationalist, has made wide use of women in his wartime buildup. During the Iraq-Iran war, he used the

General Federation of Iraqi Women to channel women into nontraditional jobs in order to free men to fight.

A Saudi feminist stationed with the United Nations in Baghdad during that war has even wondered aloud whether it didn't further Iraqi women's emancipation. The more devastating the conflict became, she recalled, the more Saddam's all-male Revolutionary Council called on women to lend their efforts to the nation (though never forsaking their primary responsibility of producing more children). Her puzzle would sound familiar to many American feminists. The U.S. government followed the same course during World War II. Of course, as the Iraqi cousins of "Rosie the Riveter" also discovered, once the war ended male government officials—and Iraqi fathers and husbands—expected women to return to the domestic feminized roles that bolstered male egos and made space for demobilized male soldiers on the production line.

Today the Iraqi Women's Federation is again being called to mobilize women, this time to put into place the consumer rationing programs that will be key to the Saddam regime's ability to withstand the U.N. embargo. It wouldn't be surprising if many Iraqi women activists saw in the crisis yet another opportunity to use wartime mobilization to demonstrate their public capabilities. Now, however, in his search for Muslim allies, Saddam is beginning to refer to his campaign as a holy cause. The more he couches his brand of Arab nationalism in religious terms, the less likely even the exigencies of wartime will produce short-term gains for Iraqi women.

There are reports out of Saudi Arabia that King Fahd has instructed his ministries to encourage Saudi women to volunteer for war-related jobs until now closed to them. Saudi women nurses who have been restricted to caring for women patients are now permitted to attend male patients. Though the Western media is heralding this announcement as evidence that mobilization may benefit the "benighted" Saudi women, there has been scarce curiosity about the history or current thinking of those women.

In fact, American coverage of the Gulf crisis has been framed by a contrast between the liberated American woman soldier and the veiled Arab woman. There is a strikingly consistent media preoccupation with the century-old Western literary tradition of "Orientalism," that package of often ambivalent ideas about the presumed backwardness yet allure of Arab culture. The harem has always been at the center of Western writers' preoccupation. In the past it was the daring Victorian lady traveler who posed the stark contrast with the secluded Arab woman. The former's presence reassured the self-satisfied Western man that his society was the more "civilized" and thus within its natural rights in colonizing the Middle East. The European woman traveler also tempted many of her homebound sisters to imagine that they were far more emancipated than they really were: Even if they were denied the vote, or couldn't divorce a violent husband, at least they weren't pent up in a harem. The imperialist enterprise relied on both Western women and men feeling superior to the patriarchal Arabs.

Today, the television and print journalists are substituting the American woman soldier for the Victorian lady traveler, but the political intent remains much the same. By contrasting the allegedly liberated American woman tank mechanic with the Saudi woman deprived of a driver's license, American reporters are implying that the United States is the advanced civilized country whose duty it is to take the lead in resolving the Persian Gulf crisis. Women of both countries are being turned into the currency with which men attempt to maintain the unequal relations between their societies.

Yet Arab women, even in the conservative societies of the Gulf, are more than passive victims of purdah. There are Saudi women who have a university education, have founded women-only banks, practice medicine in women-only hospitals, earn wages in newly-established garment factories. One need not overstate the political and economic freedom of these women to argue that Saudi women are diverse and have authentic analyses of their own political and social situation.

There are Kuwaiti women who have organized neighborhood-level protests against the occupying Iraqi army. Susan Shuaib, a Kuwaiti-British feminist writing in *New Statesman and Society,* puts this surprising news in the broader context of Kuwait's changing political relations between women and men. Just this July, according to Shuaib, women had become more visible as activists pressing for parliamentary government. They organized petition drives and took part in public rallies.

The second problem with the neo-Orientalist interpretation adopted by so many American reporters is that it measures American women soldiers' "advances" outside any consideration of militarism. Approximately 11 percent of all the U.S. forces in Saudi Arabia are women, matching their proportions in the military as a whole. In the American media, the woman flying a giant C-141 transportation plane is portrayed as the natural descendant of Susan B. Anthony.

It's true that many American women in the military do see themselves as feminists, breaking down formidable sexist barriers. For them, the Persian Gulf operation is not part of the Middle East's political evolution; it is part of a political struggle that began with the American women in Vietnam, and was carried into the U.S. invasions of Grenada and Panama. Each U.S. military intervention has provided women with a chance to hone their bureaucratic skills, perfect end runs around chauvanist field commanders, and turn up the heat on those Pentagon officials still dragging their feet in opening up military career opportunities to women soldiers.

If, however, winning "first-class citizenship" depends on American women gaining full acceptance in the military, what does that say about the very meaning of citizenship? In all the coverage of American women soldiers' gains, there is the implication that the military defines citizenship.

The always artificial categories of "combat," "near combat," and "noncombat" may indeed be crumbling in the desert. But few women are talking yet about what sorts of sexual harassment they are likely to experience as the weeks pass and our soldiers have none of their usual access to foreign women overseas. (Which country will play host to the thousands of American soldiers on "R & R"? Not Saudi Arabia. Whichever government agrees to serve as a rest and recreation site will make agreements with the Pentagon to insure that American male soldiers will have direct access to local women without endangering the men's health. Buried in the fine print of government-to-government R & R agreements are stipulations about public health and police authority that directly affect women's relations with GIs.) According to the Pentagon's own recently released study, 64 percent of women in the military say they have been sexually harassed. A woman soldier who won't pay attention to a male colleague is always vulnerable to lesbian baiting. But this is made doubly intimidating when the Pentagon persists in its policy of forcing suspected lesbians out of service.

The Persian Gulf crisis is not built out of relations among ungendered presidents, foreign ministers, oil executives, and soldiers. If we pay attention to the experiences and ideas of the various women involved, two realities come into sharper focus. First, this international confrontation, like others before it, is played out in part by governments attempting to confine women in roles that, even when they briefly shake conventional social norms, nonetheless serve those governments' interests. Second, men's sense of their own masculinity, often tenuous, is as much a factor in international politics as the flow of oil, cables, or military hardware.

Part II
Seizing Opportunities
For Change

Failure to Quit

Is Activism Worth It?

Howard Zinn

How can one hope to organize against something as big and devastating as a war? What is the point of trying to create fundamental social change that would prevent war in the future? As Howard Zinn makes clear, resistance to war did not begin on the day following George Bush's assignment of troops to Saudi Arabia. Rather, the struggle for peace and justice has strong historical roots. Recalling some of the successes can give us the strength needed to persevere.

I can understand pessimism, but I don't believe in it. It's not simply a matter of faith, but of historical evidence. Not overwhelming evidence, just enough to give hope, because for hope we don't need certainty, only possibility. Despite all those confident statements that "history shows..." and "history proves...," hope is all the past can offer us.

When I hear so often that there is little hope for change in the '90s, I think back to the despair that accompanied the onset of the '60s.

Historians of the late '40s and '50s (Richard Hofstadter, Louis Hartz) were writing ruefully about a liberal-conservative "consensus" that dominated the United States all through its history and that still prevailed, setting severe limits to change. Herbert Marcuse, at the start of the '60s, saw American society, American thought, as "one-dimensional," with radical ideas absorbed and deflected, dissent repressed through "tolerance."

One could not read these men, socially conscious, desirous themselves of change yet despairing of it, without feeling a deep pessimism about the possibilities for change in the United States. As the year 1960 began, Princeton philosopher Walter Kaufmann lamented the "uncommitted generation" and wrote: "What distinguishes them is that they are not committed to any cause." Neither he nor Hofstadter, Hartz, Marcuse, nor anyone for that matter, could have foreseen what would soon happen. It was unprecedented, unpredicted, and for at least fifteen years, uncontrollable. It would shake the country and startle the world, with consequences we are hardly aware of today.

True, those consequences did not include the end of war, exploitation, hunger, racism, military intervention, nationalism, sexism—only the end of legal racial segregation, the end of the war in Vietnam, the end of illegal abortions. It was just a beginning.

The age of apathy? I thought so too when, out of the Air Force, married, with two small children, finishing graduate work in history at Columbia University, I went south to teach in Atlanta, Georgia. My job was at Spelman College, where young black women, the daughters of railroad porters, teachers, ministers, maids, laborers, and farmers, came to get their degrees. It was 1956. The atmosphere on that tree-lined, fragrant campus was sedate, quiet, careful, and only close attention to what was said and left unsaid revealed deep resentment just below the surface. By 1960, these same quiet students were sitting in, demonstrating, picketing, going to jail. I learned that it was a serious mistake to interpret lack of action as lack of thought, lack of feeling. Rather, it was the absence of opportunities, openings, examples to emulate, groups to join—but when those appeared, the silence changed to uproar.

With the Gulf crisis there is an uproar that reaches beyond the student constituency into a much broader resistance to war. But just as other authors in this anthology make clear that the Gulf crisis did not spring out of nowhere but rather was the product of many years of strife to which the United States contributed, so too it is clear that the activism that has risen against U.S. policies is the product of years of struggle. Resistance to war today is broadly based, and has significant new elements in it. The Military Families Support Network is one example of this dynamic creativity. We are not out to shame the soldiers. We are helping them to resist.

Before the Gulf crisis there was much talk about the silence of the '80s. That silence deserves attention. In 1984 there was a silent majority in this country that refused to vote for Reagan: 68 percent of the eligible voters (add 21 percent who voted for Mondale with the 47 percent who didn't bother to vote). The unimpressive 32 percent who voted for Reagan was converted by a timid press and gullible public into an "overwhelming mandate." Four years later, in 1988, a majority of voters again refused to vote for Bush by similar margins.

But there is more than silence.

There is a human carry-over from the '60s. True, there are some veterans of those movements who have surrendered radical priorities for conventional "success." But there are others looking for openings and opportunities, pushing the system to its limits while pointing beyond, keeping the spirit of resistance alive. Many have been working steadily on various issues of peace and justice, leading up to the present feverish activity over war in the Persian Gulf.

I think of my students at Spelman, among the many who were jailed during the Atlanta sit-ins: Marian Wright, going to Yale Law School, and to Mississippi with the Movement, now the tireless head of the Children's Defense Fund in Washington; Alice Walker, becoming a poet, a novelist, a feminist and political activist. I think of Carolyn Mugar, working with anti-war GIs in the Viet-

nam years, more recently a labor organizer in southern
Massachusetts. Or Bernice Johnson Reagon, student
leader and Freedom Singer in the Albany, Georgia Movement of 1961-62, now a curator at the Smithsonian Institution, National Museum of American History, a
formidable mind and voice, still a Freedom Singer ("Sweet
Honey in the Rock"). And Staughton Lynd, historian,
organizer of Freedom Schools in Mississippi, anti-war
protester of the '60s, now a labor lawyer in Ohio.

We all know such people, but it goes far beyond
personal connections. There are thousands of local groups
around the country—many more than existed in the
'60s—devoted to struggling for tenants' rights or women's
rights, or environmental protection, or against the arms
race, or to take care of the hungry and homeless, or those
in need of health care. There are now tens of thousands of
professionals, many of them veterans of the movements
of the '60s, who bring unorthodox ideas and humane
values into courtrooms, classrooms, and hospitals.

Several years ago, when Reagan announced the
blockade of Nicaragua, 550 of us sat in at the federal
building in Boston to protest, and were arrested. It
seemed too big a group of dissidents to deal with, and
charges were dropped. The official complaint against all
of us was: "Failure to Quit." That is, surely, the critical
fact about the continuing movement for human rights
here and all over the world.

Activism has worked. Over 50,000 people signed the
Pledge of Resistance, committing themselves to protest
against the U.S. intervention in Central America. A small
number, but it represents a large part of the nation,
because survey after survey has shown a majority of the
country opposed to administration policy in Central
America. True the quick invasion of Panama met with
little resistance. But is it not reasonable to assume that a
U.S. invasion of Nicaragua, so lusted after by the Reagan
Administration, was forestalled by recognition that the

public would not support such an action? Congress, timid as it was, still had to respond to public opinion.

During the Iran-contra hearings, Oliver North chastised Congress repeatedly for not standing behind the president's policy in Nicaragua. Senator Patrick Leahy of Vermont, in exasperation, replied that Congress had no choice—mail was running so heavily against aid to the contras and invading Nicaragua that Congress didn't dare support Reagan's policy. Reagan's support for the contras was forced to become clandestine, and though enough havoc was created in Nicaragua to defeat the Sandinistas in the election, they have survived as an important force in the new situation.

When activists have committed civil disobedience to protest Central American policy, or the CIA, or the arms race, or U.S. actions in the Middle East, the degree of their support in the general public can be measured, at least roughly, by how juries of ordinary citizens react. During the war in Vietnam, when religious pacifists entered draft boards illegally to destroy draft records as a way of protesting the war, juries became incresingly reluctant to convict, and near the end of the war we saw the dramatic acquittal of the Camden 28 by a jury which then threw a party for the defendants.

Acts of civil disobedience during the '80s, at a much earlier stage of U.S. intervention than that in Vietnam, brought verdicts of acquittal whenever juries were permitted to listen to the defendants' reasons for their civil disobedience. In the spring of 1984, in Burlington, Vermont, the "Winooski 44" had occupied Senator Stafford's office to protest his support of aid to the contras. The jury, after hearing many hours of testimony about conditions in Nicaragua, the role of the CIA, and the nature of the contras, voted for acquittal. One of the jurors, a local house painter, said: "I was honored to be on that jury. I felt a part of history."

In Minneapolis that same year, seven "trespassers"

protesting at the Honeywell Corporation were acquitted. In 1985, men and women blocked the Great Lakes Training Station in Illinois, others blocked the South African Embassy in Chicago, nineteen people in the state of Washington halted trains carrying warheads, and all these won acquittals in court. In western Massachusetts, where a protest against the CIA took place, there was another surprising acquittal. One of the jurors, Donna L. Moody, told a reporter: "All the expert testimony against the CIA was alarming. It was very educational."

Over the past six years, eighteen "Plowshares" actions, involving symbolic sabotage of nuclear weaponry, have resulted mostly in guilty verdicts. In the latest case, involving two Catholic priests and two others who broke into a naval air station near Philadelphia and damaged three aircraft, the judge refused the defense of "necessity" but allowed the jury to hear the defendants' reasons for their actions. The jury was unable to reach a verdict.

We hear many glib dismissals of today's college students and professionals as being totally preoccupied with money and self. There is obvious concern among students with their economic futures—evidence of the failure of the economic system to provide for the young, more than a sign of their indifference to social injustice. Still, the past few years have seen political actions on campuses all over the country. For 1986 alone, a partial list shows: 182 students calling for divestment from South Africa, arrested at the University of Texas; a black-tie dinner for alumni at Harvard called off after a protest on South African holdings; charges dropped against 49 Wellesley protesters after half the campus boycotted classes in support; and more protests recorded at Yale, Wisconsin, Louisville, San Jose, Columbia.

The activist message of "no more war," reflected in a divided public, has caused Bush to rush from one explanation to another in defending his Persian Gulf policy. In desperation, he keeps comparing Saddam Hussein to Hitler, trying to rekindle the popular support the government had in World War II. His outright promise in a press conference on December 4 that the Gulf crisis "would not be another Vietnam" is an acknowledgement of the deeply ingrained aversion to war that is a legacy of that terrible adventure.

There has been a quick emergence of military resistance in the latest crisis. For instance, Marine Corporal Erik Larsen has eloquently put Bush's Gulf policy in a larger perspective. He explains his refusal to participate in a Gulf war elsewhere in this book.

But what about the others, the non-protesting students? Here, too, we must not underestimate the potential for change. Among the liberal arts students, business majors, and ROTC cadets in my classes, there have been super-patriots and enthusiasts of capitalism, but also others whose thoughts deserve some attention:

Writing in his class journal, one ROTC student, whose father was a navy flier, his brother a navy commander: "This one class made me go out and read up on South Africa. What I learned made me sick. My entire semester has been a paradox. I go to your class and I see a Vietnam vet named Joe Bangert tell of his experiences in the war. I was enthralled by his talk...By the end of that hour and a half, I hated the Vietnam War as much as he did. The only problem is that three hours after class I am marching around in my uniform—and feeling great about it. Is there something wrong with me? Am I being hypocritical? Sometimes I don't know..."

A young woman in ROTC: "What really stuck in my mind was the ignorance some people displayed at the end of class. We were discussing welfare. Some students stated that people on welfare were lazy, that if they really wanted to, they could find jobs. Argg! These rich kids (or middle class or whatever) who have all they need think they are so superior it makes me angry..."

The same student, after seeing the film *Hearts and*

Minds: "General Westmoreland said 'Orientals don't value lives.' I was incredulous. And then they showed the little boy holding the picture of his father and he was crying and crying and crying... I must admit I started crying. What's worse was that I was wearing my Army uniform that day and I had to make a conscious effort not to disappear into my seat."

A young woman in the School of Management: "North broke the law, but will he be punished?...if he is let off the hook then all of America is punished. Every inner-city kid who is sent to jail for stealing food to feed his brothers and sisters is punished. Every elderly person who has to fight just to keep warm on a winter night will be punished...The law is supposed to be the common bond—the peace-making body. Yet it only serves the function selectively—just when the people in control wish it to."

Surely history does not start anew with each decade. The roots of one era branch and flower in subsequent eras. Human beings, writings, invisible transmitters of all kinds, carry messages across the generations. I try to be pessimistic, to keep up with some of my friends. But I think back over the decades, and look around. And then it seems to me that the future is not certain, but it is possible.

The Persian Gulf Crisis and Opportunities for Social Change

Stephen Zunes

In organizing against war, both in the short- and long-term, how can we move toward creating change? As Zunes argues, several agenda items are important stepping stones. These include supporting national self-determination, strengthening the United Nations, promoting nuclear nonproliferation and disarmament, challenging militarism, supporting democracy in the third world, and creating an energy policy based on safe, renewable resources. He makes a strong case that activists must not get lulled into thinking they are on the fringe of society in their desire for peace and justice, but are faced with new opportunities to build broad coalitions for change.

The Chinese character for "crisis" is a compound word, combining the characters for "danger" and "opportunity." It is in this light that activists should view the Persian Gulf crisis. The dangers are fairly obvious, not just from the carnage of a general war but from the risk that the outcome will be a triumph for militarism, interventionism, and the national security state. A perception of the successful use of U.S. military force in the Middle East could lead to a new militarism and a precedent for further interventions on even less legitimate pretexts. Continued high military spending to maintain such a capability would mean that domestic programs would be drastically sacrificed to reduce the federal deficit. Anti-

Arab racism could reach epidemic proportions, not only making things difficult for Arab Americans, but further postponing national self-determination for the Palestinians, as the U.S. government continues to deny the same basic rights for the Arabs of the former British mandate that it guarantees for the Jews. Increased U.S. assistance to Israel and to reactionary Arab states could be further legitimized, as would a permanent U.S. military presence in the region, at enormous cost to the American taxpayer and to the sovereignty of Middle Eastern countries. The impact on oil prices may lead to a resurgence of the nuclear power industry and the opening of new oil drilling in the Arctic National Wildlife Refuge and fragile coastal areas. The Democratic Party would become even more timid in challenging the direction of American foreign policy. Indeed, "successful" use of military force would mean that many of the goals for which progressive movements have struggled during the past two decades would be seriously threatened.

The opportunities the current crisis presents must be appreciated as well, however, since if utilized to our benefit, they could lead to progress on a number of important areas of concern. There are some key areas where anti-war activists can build on the growing resentment to U.S. Middle East policy to create a major movement for fundamental changes in United States foreign and domestic policy. These include the following:

Support for National Self-Determination

The stated willingness by the United States government to sacrifice thousands of American lives and to spend billions of dollars for the cause of Kuwaiti national self-determination opens the door to publicize the plight of other countries currently suffering under foreign occupation, particularly those where the occupying armies are being funded by the United States. Areas under Israeli occupation—the West Bank, the Gaza Strip, the Golan Heights, and southern Lebanon—are the most obvious, given the fact that Israel is the largest recipient of U.S. foreign aid and that the occupation forces are absolutely dependent on that aid in order to maintain their costly control over an increasingly hostile population. The often-stated U.S. opposition to Palestinian self-determination is indicative of the enormous hypocrisy of current Middle East policy, a double standard that is now being taken to task by the United States' Arab allies and others. The wrongheaded but understandable early Palestinian support of Iraq, brought on by their resentment over the U.S. refusal to respond positively to significant peace overtures by the Palestine Liberation Organization, led some Americans to question once again Palestinian statehood—though if questionable alliances negated a people's right to national self-determination, Israel would not exist either. However, this initial pro-Iraqi fervor has died down considerably since reports from Palestinians living in Kuwait have told of the brutality of the Iraqi occupation. Palestinians know better than most people what it is like to live under the gun of a conquering army.

The Palestinians have repeatedly suffered from the transgressions of Arab dictators: attacks by neighboring Arab states against Israel upon its creation in 1948 led to the forced exodus by triumphant Israeli forces of most of the Palestinian population, expanding Israel's borders well beyond the boundaries established by the United Nations partition. Both Jordan and Egypt took over the designated Palestinian areas, thereby denying the Palestinians the state promised to them by the world community. Nasser's threats in 1967 led Israel to launch its pre-emptive strike which placed the remaining Arab parts of Palestine—the West Bank and Gaza Strip—under an Israeli military occupation which remains to this day. Subsequently, when moderates in the Palestine Liberation Organization—Said Hammami, Issam Sartawi and others—have spoken out for peace with Israel, they have been victims of assassination by extremists backed by Iraq, Syria, or Libya. Whenever the dominant moderate groups in the PLO have begun to make diplomatic progress, Palestinian terrorists—backed by these same governments—have derailed the peace process through violence. This pattern is no accident: Arab states have traditionally used the Palestinians as pawns for their own political purposes. Israel's history of mistreatment of the Palestinians has been used as an excuse to divert the attention and frustrations of other Arabs away from the misrule by their own leaders and towards the Jewish state. A just peace—recognizing the rights of both Israeli Jews and Palestinian Arabs to their own homeland—would deny Arab dictators such a target.

It would also deny Saddam Hussein the glaring Western double standard as an excuse for his own acts of aggression. His disingenuous insistence on linking Iraq's withdrawal from Kuwait with Israeli withdrawal from Arab territories has struck a powerful chord for millions of Arabs. Therefore, on both moral and practical grounds, activists must insist that the U.S. government acknowledge that the Palestinians have as much right to choose their own government and to be free from foreign military occupation as do the Kuwaitis, and insure that U.S. pressure on Israel must increase, not lessen, for a negotiated end to Israeli control of its occupied territories. If done carefully, these issues can be pressed in a manner which does not unduly alarm those concerned with Israel's survival in a hostile Middle East and still bring justice to the long-suffering Palestinian people.

There are also other U.S. allies occupying neighboring states. Since 1974, Turkey, a member of NATO, has occupied the northern third of Cyprus, when it forcibly expelled the entire ethnic Greek majority and set up a puppet government. Congress cut off aid to Turkey for three years following the invasion, only to restore it following vigorous lobbying by the Carter administration, despite the absence of any compromise on the part of the Turks. Turkey also continues to occupy what was once part of Armenia and Kurdistan; the Armenian population was physically eliminated—over one million were massacred 75 years ago—and the Kurds continue to be denied basic cultural and political rights. Already the third largest recipient of U.S. foreign aid, Turkey—due to its strategic location on Iraq's northwestern border—has been the recipient of an increased amount of U.S. foreign aid in recent months, despite its own occupations and human rights violations.

In 1975, Morocco, another close U.S. ally, invaded the Western Sahara, a Spanish colony on the verge of independence, driving out most of the population and severely repressing those remaining. Morocco's King Hassan annexed the territory and embarked on a massive colonization effort, bringing tens of thousands of Moroccans into the region. The Western Sahara government, known formally as the Sahrawi Arab Democratic Republic, is a full member of the Organization for African Unity and is recognized by more than seventy nations. The SADR, through the Polisario Front, governs the majority of Sahrawis that live in a series of refugee camps in the Algerian desert, and has been waging a guerrilla war against the Moroccan occupation forces. Despite a U.S. law that specifically bans military aid to Morocco being used outside its internationally recognized borders, U.S. assistance to Morocco dramatically increased following the invasion, and arms to the occupation forces continue to flow at high levels.

Also in 1975, Indonesia invaded and annexed the newly-independent island nation of East Timor, sealed it off from the outside world and embarked upon a systematic slaughter of the Timorese, with some estimates ranging as high as 200,000 people—one-third of the country's population. U.S. military aid immediately shot up by 79

percent, consisting largely of counter-insurgency weaponry to support the occupation forces. Indonesians have
been colonizing the former Portuguese colony at a rapid
pace, and the repression has essentially eliminated any
organized nationalist activity. A recent *New York Times*
editorial strongly chastised the U.S. double standard on
military occupations with reference to East Timor,
which—given the newspaper's poor coverage of the issue
until then—is indicative of a new sensitivity to the fate of
other countries sharing Kuwait's tragedy.

The widespread and highly justifiable public sympathy for the plight of the Kuwaitis provides an important
opportunity to mobilize support for other peoples under
occupation and to challenge U.S. policies which maintain
these occupations. If the new world order is really to lead
to a strict adherence to international law regarding the
inviolability of international boundaries and the right of
national self-determination, then the United States must
respond to these other violations as well. This will only
occur if activists are willing to make them an issue.

Strengthening the United Nations

With each of these cases, as well as with the formerly
South African-occupied Namibia, which won its independence just last year, the United States has effectively
blocked decisive action by the United Nations. It is therefore particularly ironic that supporters of U.S. Persian
Gulf policy are using the failure of sanctions in the past
as a reason why they should not be given time to take
effect against Iraq. It also raises serious questions regarding the U.S. claim to be the world's primary enforcer of
international law. Not only has the United States blocked
the imposition of sanctions in the above cases, but the
United States openly defied United Nations sanctions in
effect against Rhodesia for most of the 1970s by importing
chrome from the illegal white minority government. In-

deed, the most flagrant violation of U.N. resolutions and rulings immediately prior to Iraq's refusal to comply with the U.N. Security Council resolutions on Kuwait was when the U.S. defied the International Court of Justice, (the U.N. judicial wing) calling for the U.S. to halt its attacks against Nicaragua and its support of the contras, and to pay financial restitution to the Sandinista government. A stronger United Nations would mean a greater opportunity for enforcement of international law against violations by Iraq, the United States, or any other government.

The U.N. has not been as supportive of United States policy in the Persian Gulf as the Bush administration and the media have implied. The U.N. has not approved the placement of U.S. ground forces in the Middle East, and the United States refuses to place its troops under United Nations command. Despite giving approval to the use of force as a means of insuring Iraqi withdrawal from Kuwait, it is highly unlikely that offensive military action would be possible were forces dependent upon decisions of the U.N. Security Council. Though some of the recent U.N. resolutions parallel U.S. policy, they were usually voted upon only after the United States made unilateral decisions—decisions made behind closed doors between the president and a handful of advisers.

Meanwhile, the United Nations' strong stand against Iraqi aggression has given the U.N. the greatest credibility in the eyes of the American public since the heyday of U.S. support in the 1950s. Progressives should use the opportunity to strengthen such support further. Long a favorite cause of liberals, many on the left have been skeptical of the United Nations, noting how the U.N. is only as good as the governments of its member states. Yet in striving for consensus among disparate nations, the U.N. can curb the potential for unilateralism by the United States and other powers with interventionary capabilities.

In a post-Cold War world, the United Nations may be the only external means by which to stop widespread U.S. intervention in the third world. Without Soviet military power as a deterrent, the moral persuasion of the world community is needed to curb the potential abuses resulting from the U.S. being the sole military superpower. There is certainly no guarantee that the U.N. will live up to its responsibilities; while the Soviet Union's support of third world nationalism may have been opportunistic in the past, its increasing dependency on the West for survival may soon render such support nonexistent. Similarly, the Chinese leadership, whose foreign policies in recent decades have been nothing short of reactionary, cannot be counted upon to challenge U.S. policy, since they expect continued American economic support despite the aging leadership's repression of Tibetans and their own dissidents.

Despite all this, however, a strong United Nations is preferable to a weak United Nations. Though the record has been mixed, the U.N., with its third world majority, has generally upheld principles of human rights, non-intervention, national self-determination, and economic justice. Activists must be willing to mobilize for greater power for the United Nations as an alternative to American unilateralism. International law, like civil liberties at home, is not enough in itself to create a just system. However, it is a necessary prerequisite.

Supporting Nuclear Nonproliferation and Disarmament

Another opportunity for activists is in strengthening the U.S. commitment to nuclear non-proliferation. The Bush administration started making exaggerated and alarmist declarations regarding Iraqi nuclear capability soon after a nationwide public opinion poll indicated that preventing Iraq from obtaining nuclear weapons was the only justification for which a majority of Americans would support going to war. (While most analysts—including Israelis, who presumably have the most to worry about—believe that Iraq will not possess nuclear weapons for at least five years, the Bush administration was claiming the Iraqis could possess the Bomb within months. The administration has not released any evidence supporting this conclusion, however.) Saddam Hussein's repeated calls for a nuclear-free zone in the Middle East have been rejected by the United States and Israel. The U.S. position has been that while it is legitimate for the United States and its allies to have nuclear weapons in the region, Iraq cannot. It is of no surprise that Iraq does not accept such unilateral terms.

Peace activists must capitalize on concerns about the spread of nuclear weapons to encourage the United States to strengthen international nonproliferation agreements which, after some half-hearted efforts by the Carter administration in the late 1970s, were subsequently abandoned. The United States in recent years has refused to support strict enforcement regarding the transfer of nuclear technology, and continues to maintain close military relationships with several countries which have refused to sign the Nuclear Nonproliferation Treaty (NPT) and which clearly have an interest in obtaining nuclear weapons.

The existing treaty not only attempts to limit the spread of nuclear weapons among lesser powers, but also calls upon countries like the United States, which already have vast nuclear arsenals, to substantially reduce their weapons stockpiles. A strict enforcement of the NPT would not only prevent the likes of Saddam Hussein from procuring nuclear weapons, but could also force substantial nuclear disarmament by the United States and other nuclear powers as well. For the United States to hold a vast nuclear stockpile and to continue to add to this arsenal despite the end of the Cold War, while at the same time threatening a major war over the prospect of a third world country procuring a single weapon, is a tenuous position worth challenging.

In addition, as with other foreign policy double standards unveiled by the current crisis, this can also allow activists to challenge U.S. support of its allies with nuclear capability or designs, such as Israel and Pakistan. Also, the demands for nonproliferation must escalate to include an end to the export of nuclear power plants, a step not only necessary to limit the spread of the fuel needed for nuclear weapons, but to halt the expansion of a very real environmental threat. Allowing the use of military force because a country might be developing nuclear weapons could lead to a breakdown of international order, and possible use of nuclear weapons; by contrast, utilizing existing and strengthened international agreements could remove the nuclear threat from the planet permanently.

Challenging Militarism

What has been striking about the negative public reaction to U.S. Persian Gulf policy is that it comes not out of any sympathy for the other side, but from a clear opposition to war itself. While some of this is of a pacifist nature, more of it is a manifestation of a widespread and growing perception among Americans of the declining utility of warfare as a means of exerting political power. As invading armies have seen repeatedly in recent decades, extraordinary advantages in forces and materiel do not necessarily ensure victory. The defeats of the United States in Vietnam and the Soviets in Afghanistan, Iraq's failed invasion of Iran, and Israel's problems in Lebanon have all served as reminders that wars can end up very differently than military strategists suppose. Meanwhile, the dramatic upsurge in the use of nonviolent action by dissatisfied populations to overthrow dictatorships from the Philippines to Czechoslovakia have demonstrated the power of non-military means of political coercion from within.

The discomfort Americans were feeling about the prospects of a major war was evident early in the crisis. It was clear this would not be like Panama or Grenada, which proved to be popular interventions in large part because of their brevity and low cost in American lives. The numbers and experience of Iraqi forces, combined with their relatively sophisticated arsenal, brought up concerns over the prospect of American casualties of an unprecedented scale. In addition, the numbers of civilian lives that will be lost brought mainstream religious leaders to question the morality of such an action. For those concentrating on pragmatic arguments, the crisis raised serious questions—however legitimate the concerns about Iraqi aggressions, existing and potential, might be—over whether it was worth the enormous amount of casualties that would result. Modern weapons have brought the human costs of war to such heights that it has made pacifism, or at least opposition to war, respectable again.

The current crisis, then, provides for the building of a genuine anti-war movement, which does not question which side the United States is on, but instead questions both the morality and rationality of war. If war cannot be justified to challenge a brutal and aggressive dictatorship like Saddam Hussein's Iraq, it is hard to foresee any realistic circumstance in which the United States can justifiably go to war at all. The political implications of this phenomenon are profound, for it questions the very basis for the United States to maintain its vast military establishment. Activists must clearly question the basic assumptions regarding a military solution to the conflict, and then extend these arguments to militarism in general.

Supporting Democracy
in the Third World

The gross violations of human rights by Saddam Hussein's regime, both in Iraqi-occupied Kuwait and within Iraq itself, have stirred the consciences of millions of Americans. However, for many years prior to the invasion of Kuwait, Middle East experts, human rights advocates and many others unsuccessfully called on the United States to get tough with the Iraqi regime. Saddam Hussein's invasion of Iran, his support of terrorism and his large-scale violations of human rights were all valid grounds for sanctions. Most significant was his use of chemical warfare against both Iranian troops and Iraq's civilian Kurdish population—the first major use of these illegal weapons since World War I. The response of the world's nations was a major test as to whether international law would be upheld through the imposition of stringent sanctions to challenge this dangerous precedent. The United States, and much of the world community, failed the test.

The U.S. Navy defended tankers and other Persian Gulf ships supporting the Iraqi war effort, despite Iraq having attacked twice as many ships as had Iran, including the U.S. Navy frigate *Stark,* which resulted in the deaths of 38 American sailors. U.S. agricultural subsidies and other economic aid flowed into Iraq. The United States sent an untold amount of indirect aid—through other Arab countries—which enabled Iraq to receive weapons and technology to increase its war-making capacity. As with Panamanian dictator Manuel Noriega, a repressive regime was quietly backed by the U.S. administration, only to tell the American people later that the "only way" to effectively respond to the regime was through military force. This pattern of U.S. policy is quite vulnerable to challenge, as are other implications of supporting such notorious regimes.

Meanwhile, despite worldwide trends towards democracy, the United States has helped perpetuate the rule of feudal monarchs in the Persian Gulf through billions of dollars in military sales and generous arrangements for economic investments. Many Arabs see these corrupt royal families as even worse than Saddam Hussein, and were not sorry to see the Kuwaiti government fall. Had the United States encouraged reform rather than an archaic and undemocratic status quo, the Arab world likely would be in a much stronger position to unite and challenge potential Iraqi aggression by itself. There already has been a lot of concern regarding the wisdom of sacrificing American lives to defend feudal monarchies, particularly Saudi Arabia, a country with no constitution and no legislature, where hundreds of people are held as political prisoners and torture is widespread, and where women are treated as chattel. Activists must raise the issue as to whether these are the kind of governments the U.S. should continue supporting, and whether these are governments worth dying for.

In addition, we need to challenge a U.S. policy which continues to support several governments rivaling Saddam Hussein's in brutality. In Latin America, Africa, and Asia, the United States sends billions of dollars' worth of economic and military aid to regimes—some with democratic facades, others, unabashed dictatorships—which deny even the most basic liberties and systematically terrorize their populations. U.S. backing of such regimes is highly unpopular. President Carter's "human rights policy," though limited largely to rhetoric, was nevertheless well-received by the American public; popular opposition to Carter's overall foreign policy was due more to its vacillations than to its alleged idealism. Not only are there serious moral questions regarding having authoritarian regimes as allies, but the Iraqi and Panamanian cases underscore the pragmatic issues as well—such dictatorships can quickly turn against our interests. Both arguments must be seized upon, since the skepticism of the American public towards U.S. alliances with such governments is at an unprecedented level.

Restructuring Budget Priorities

The cost of maintaining a large U.S. military presence in the Middle East is enormous. No matter who ends up footing the bill, the debate can be put to the advantage of progressive activists. The major cutbacks and minor tax increases facing Americans make it easy to utilize guns-versus-butter arguments. Is the deployment of hundreds of thousands of American troops in the Middle East—which may last well beyond the end of the war with Iraq—really worth the resulting cutbacks in student loans, low-income housing, farm subsidies, public transit, and medical care? Never has the public been more receptive to populist arguments regarding budget priorities, given the end of the Cold War combined with a huge national debt, a decaying infrastructure, and a serious recession. In addition, the absence of reservists called into active duty has depleted needed workers for small businesses and certain specialized services and trades, creating additional economic hardship in certain areas.

High military spending does more damage to the economy than simply taking money from current needed domestic programs and mortgaging such programs for the future: it has an inflationary effect by producing items not circulated within the economy; it increases the balance of trade deficit by shipping equipment and personnel abroad; it increases unemployment by being the least labor-intensive major program of the federal government; it shifts income from more productive small businesses towards existing conglomerates; and it damages U.S. economic competitiveness by focusing research programs and the energies of scientists and engineers away from consumer technologies towards the military sphere.

If somehow the Saudis, Japanese, or other allies do end up paying for the cost of the war, activists can raise other questions: have the U.S. armed forces simply become mercenaries of a new world order? Are we just modern-day Hessians in a global capitalist division-of-labor, where the Japanese export the new consumer technologies and we export the Marines? While the United States carries by far the highest military budget in the world and military projects use up most government research and development money, the relatively non-militarized economies of Japan and the European Community are pulling way ahead. These growing economies can then use the United States as a "rent-a-cop" when their sources of oil are threatened. (Indeed, the Japanese and Europeans are far more dependent on the Persian Gulf for their oil supplies than is the United States.) A healthy form of nationalism can be encouraged to raise fundamental questions about the U.S. role in the world and the direction of our economy.

Creating a New Energy Policy Based on Safe Renewable Sources

The Persian Gulf crisis has once again highlighted U.S. dependence on imported oil. Activists need to publicize the fact that there are alternatives to dependence on imported oil that do not endanger the environment. These include decentralized and renewable energy sources as solar, biomass, wind, geothermal, and small-scale hydropower. The technology is already available to produce these commercially, yet they have not proved "viable" because they tend not to benefit large corporations, and therefore have not received the billions of dollars' worth of subsidies as have other forms of energy production.

The nuclear power industry, for example, has benefited from nearly 40 years of taxpayer-funded research

and development. Government agencies have advocated
its adoption, bent regulatory laws in its favor, and even
insured it against liability. Currently, U.S. taxpayers are
spending millions of dollars every day to send American
troops to protect oil supplies that would not be needed if
these alternative energy sources were utilized. Indeed,
the past twenty years has seen more than $200 billion
spent on military forces designed largely to protect Middle
Eastern oil fields. If these costs were factored into what
we pay for gasoline at the pump, it might actually encourage conservation. Instead, the burden is being paid in the
form of taxes, cutbacks in needed social programs, and the
growing national debt which will have to be repaid some-
day.

Had the Reagan and Bush administrations not sus-
pended the automobile fuel efficiency standards set in the
1970s, current models would be averaging six to seven
miles per gallon higher than they are today. That is the
equivalent of all the oil we import from Iraq, Kuwait, and
Saudi Arabia combined. We need to challenge Americans
to wonder whether it would be better to spend slightly
more on a new car, or billions in military costs to insure
continued access to oil from these countries. Public opinion polls indicate widespread support—83 percent of the
American public would be willing to spend up to $500
more for a car with higher fuel efficiency.

However, both the oil companies and the Bush administration are lobbying hard against strengthening fuel
efficiency standards. In addition, government support for
mass transit, perhaps the most effective means of encouraging energy conservation, is experiencing its tenth con-
secutive year of cutbacks—public transportation receives
one-third less money from the government than it did a
decade ago. While the government subsidizes the automobile through the interstate highway system, and air travel
through its air traffic control system, support for passen-
ger trains—the most energy-efficient means of inter-city

transportation—is the lowest in the industrialized world. Recent administrations have even attempted to eliminate Amtrak altogether.

The Carter administration's energy policy was not a good model, either. Instead of stressing conservation and decentralized alternative methods, Carter's policy called for billions of dollars to develop synthetic fuels, solar satellites, power towers, and other capital-intensive methods—indeed, 80 percent of the research and development money during that era went to the energy conglomerates. Contrast that with Japan, which instead stressed conservation and decentralized solar technology. Japan's investment in a high-speed rail system has paid for itself many times over, as have conservation methods in industry. Rather than dumping billions of dollars into dubious synfuels projects or relying on market forces, they ended up saving billions instead. Japan now uses far less energy per unit of GNP than does the United States, a major reason for America's relative decline.

We need to ensure that the power of the energy conglomerates to affect governmental policy not be underestimated; noting how it is no accident that the president of the United States is a former oil company executive. We must again underscore the importance of developing an energy policy, along with a foreign policy, which places the service of the American people and the protection of the environment above that of corporate profits. There was enormous skepticism and anger by consumers over the immediate and dramatic price rise at the gas pumps following Iraq's invasion of Kuwait, which took place despite the fact that it takes 30 to 60 days for Persian Gulf oil to reach American service stations. Enormous price hikes even hit parts of the country that consume exclusively American oil. This willingness of the American people to place the blame where it belongs—on monopolistic corporations instead of on a third world people—is an opportunity to raise broader questions regarding both energy policy and the concentration of economic power in the United States.

Prospects for Change

Despite initial popular support for the war, the prospects are good for building an anti-war movement which also addresses broader social, economic, and political concerns. On the day the war broke out, the peace movement was larger than it was after more than three years of fighting by U.S. forces in Vietnam and, at its core, stronger. It is inter-generational, with new activists on the campuses joining those who have fought for peace and social justice for decades and whose personal politics and group process skills have been well-developed. The peace movement now has the support of mainstream churches and key segments of organized labor. A weaker economy means that the economic consequences of the war will be felt sooner, leading to an onrush of activism by those who bear the brunt of its effects. The tremendous gap between men and women in attitudes towards the war, detected in public opinion polls, can stimulate a growing understanding of the role of patriarchy and encourage leadership by women in the movement.

The censorship of media reports from the battle area, the threats and harassment against activists, and the enormous propaganda machinery mobilized to support U.S. policy are predictable responses to the power of the people to challenge the war system in all its manifestations. Rather than discourage us, this reaction should be seen as a validation of our strength. It will be a test of the political skills and the maturity of the movement to maintain as diverse a coalition as possible to end the war and, at the same time to build a broader progressive agenda. In this time of danger and opportunity, it is a test we cannot fail.

Creating an "Iraq Syndrome"

Denis F. Doyon

Henry Kissinger coined the term "Vietnam Syn-
drome" to describe the deep reluctance of people in the
United States to go to war after the catastrophe in Viet-
nam. That a former Secretary of State would describe a
preference for peace over war in terms usually reserved to
connote disease may give us pause for thought about the
nature of our society. But this "syndrome" has been nur-
tured by activists who understand that aversion to war is
one basis on which pressure for changing U.S. foreign
policy can be built. History, as Victor Hugo once said, is
written by the victors. If we are to succeed in moving the
United States away from a foreign policy which is rooted
in rule by force, we must not let the history of the Persian
Gulf crisis be written as a prescriptive cure for the Vietnam
Syndrome. Instead, we must expose the tragic course of the
war in the Gulf for the horror that it is and reinvigorate
public resistance to war. In short, we must create an Iraq
Syndrome. As Doyon makes clear, one key to our success
is building a diverse movement.

The U.S. movement against the war in the Gulf has
grown rapidly in the few months since the Iraqi invasion
of Kuwait on August 2, 1990. Until the war began in
January its top priority had been to restrain the Bush
administration's rush toward war and to bring the U.S.
troops home. Since the war began, the objective has been
to end it as soon as possible. Different emphases have
emerged among different sectors of the peace and justice
movement, but this is the common denominator. This
chapter will attempt to look beyond these short-term

objectives, which are examined elsewhere in this book, to examine longer-term organizing goals.

Admittedly, there has been little time to think about long-term strategy. The crisis burst onto the national agenda almost without warning; less than six months after most people in the United States first heard about Saddam Hussein, the country went to war.

As we organize to end the war, however, we should consider now the longer-term implications of how we are organizing. Calling for a ceasefire and the withdrawal of U.S. troops is an appropriate and urgent short-term objective, but it cannot be expected to sustain a movement over the long haul. Even if we succeed in stopping this war, others are sure to follow. If we seek to delegitimize war and intervention as instruments of national policy, we must do more than bring the U.S. troops home from Saudi Arabia; we must build a long-lasting, deeply-rooted aversion to war in the people of the United States.

Whether or not the anti-war movement can achieve this will depend to a great extent on how the public sees the options before us, and how it judges the choices made by our country's leaders. As this is written, it is too early to tell how the public will answer a few key questions: Was war the only choice, taken reluctantly by leaders who exhausted all other options? Or is it unnecessary and unwise? Was a diplomatic solution possible, and deliberately ignored or avoided? What will constitute victory? What will be gained, for whom, and at what cost? Is war worth it?

If there is no interference from the political establishment, the U.S. military can undoubtedly win the war against Iraq, even though the cost in human life and national treasure will be dreadful. While Iraq is a formidable military foe, the United States has unleashed massive military force on it. If all else fails, the United States can use nuclear weapons. There is little the anti-war movement can do about this objective military fact.

On the political level, however, we have more power. Now that the country has gone to war, the peace and justice movement should work to ensure that the warmakers lose. We can win the battle for the hearts and minds of the U.S. people by creating an "Iraq Syndrome," a widely-shared popular belief that the war is unnecessary, unjust, too costly, and just plain wrong. Just as the Vietnam Syndrome placed political restraints on U.S. warmaking in the 1970s and 1980s, an Iraq Syndrome might prevent future wars in the 1990s and beyond.

Building a More Diverse Movement

It is an article of faith for many peace and justice activists that we need to build a broader, more diverse movement. Some repeat the slogans with almost ritualistic ease. These slogans are "politically correct." They help activists operating in narrow, culturally homogeneous spheres to feel better about themselves.

The peace and justice movement, however, needs victories, not therapy. Building a truly multiracial, multicultural movement is not just a laudable goal; it is essential to our success. Any movement is strengthened when several communities engage in a dialog about the problems we face and jointly fashion alternatives. For the current anti-war movement, this is critical. We will not be able to create an Iraq Syndrome unless the movement includes African-Americans, Latinos, and other people of color, Arab-Americans, Jewish-Americans, the poor, women, young people, and military service personnel and their families. In addition to participating in the debate about alternatives, each of these constituencies has a particular contribution to make to a long-term movement to delegitimize war and intervention as an instrument of national policy.

War is Unnecessary

Most people in the U.S. recognize that there are real problems in the Middle East. By an overwhelming margin, they oppose Iraq's invasion and occupation of Kuwait. They worry about Iraq's chemical weapons and the threat of nuclear proliferation in the region. Thus, when the Bush administration said we must go to war to end the occupation of Kuwait and eliminate the Iraqi threat, many people agreed.

There were always alternatives to war, of course. Economic sanctions could have worked, if they had been given enough time. Intensive diplomacy could have been undertaken to secure Iraq's withdrawal from Kuwait. Negotiations can still resolve the fundamental conflicts in the Middle East. Yet for the most part, the movement against the war in the Gulf has done little to promote realistic alternatives. The common political goals seem more relevant to the U.S. public's self-interest (Troops Out Now!) than to justice in the Middle East.

This may be related to the fact that the people with the most to lose—Arabs—are not adequately represented in the leadership of the movement. At this point, none of the main national coalitions organizing grassroots response to the war include significant leadership or participation from Arab Americans. Most movement groups developed their platforms and position papers on the conflict without seeking out the perspectives of Iraqis, Kuwaitis or Saudis. Some have used blatantly racist arguments to oppose the war (for example, the line that the Kuwaitis and Saudis are all rich oil sheikhs.)

When some groups have sought to involve Arab Americans in their work, they have often reached out to Palestinians. To some degree, this reflects the successes of solidarity work and organizing efforts for Israeli/Palestinian peace. Five years ago, peace activists might not have known Palestinians in their communities; now they do. But it may also reflect a lack of appreciation for the diversity among Arabs. While Palestinians have an important role to play in the movement against a war in the Gulf, they cannot substitute for Iraqis, Kuwaitis and Saudis, any more than Mexicans can substitute for Salvadorans in the movement against U.S. intervention in Central America.

If the peace and justice movement is to develop realistic alternatives to war in the Gulf, we must involve Arabs and Arab Americans at all levels of the movement. Calls for an "Arab solution" to the Gulf crisis ring hollow when the anti-war movement itself does not provide a platform for Arabs to debate and discuss the issues.

Further, most people recognize that the Israeli/Palestinian/Arab conflict is inextricably linked to the Gulf crisis. Here we have an advantage: despite the Bush administration's best efforts to keep the occupation of the West Bank and Gaza Strip off the political agenda, the public knows that the occupation continues; news coverage of the intifada has brought it into their living rooms. Realistic proposals for resolving the Gulf crisis which acknowledge the need also to resolve the Israeli/Palestinian/Arab conflict thus stand a good chance of gathering broad public support.

This is where the participation of Palestinians—and the participation of Jewish Americans—is essential. As the primary victims of U.S. policy in the Middle East for the past several decades, Palestinians must be involved in developing a Middle East peace alternative. For an alternative to be politically viable, Israelis and Jews must also help to create it. Already, expressions of solidarity with Arabs under attack by the United States are being interpreted (in at least some cases, accurately) as solidarity against Israel, or worse, against Jews. The outbreak of war in the Middle East has encouraged both anti-Arab racism and anti-Semitism in this country; an anti-war movement which includes Arab Americans and Jewish Americans will be best equipped to confront this.

War is Unjust

War has always extracted the highest costs from the poor and oppressed, for the benefit of the rich and powerful. The war in the Gulf has simply brought these issues into sharper focus than have earlier wars. The Gulf crisis has erupted at a time of shrinking economic opportunity in the United States, after a decade of Reaganomics has succeeded in making the rich richer and the poor poorer. The all-volunteer military and the "economic draft" have led to a disproportionate representation in the military of African Americans, Latinos and other people of color, and especially poor people of all races. This is particularly true for combat units. Drive through any major city in the country; the yellow ribbons are far more numerous in poorer neighborhoods.

In similar ways, the war in the Gulf has highlighted the intersection of war and gender. Media coverage of the "women warriors" in the U.S. armed forces has questioned the country's readiness to accept women dying in battle, even though there is little outrage at women dying in the streets of our own cities. Further, the media has rarely questioned the wisdom of going to war to defend kingdoms which practice gender apartheid.

It should not be surprising, then, that poor people, people of color and women are the groups least supportive of the Bush administration's policies in the Gulf. Women have led some of the most creative responses to the war, including the Gulf Peace Team's encampment along the Iraqi-Saudi border. Some of the strongest opposition to war in the Gulf has come from leaders in the African-American community, particularly from community organizations, the churches, colleges and high schools. The Congressional Black Caucus has led opposition to the war in Congress. African-American soldiers and reservists have mounted some of the earliest and most significant resistance within the military. In many communities of color, the yellow ribbons are an expression of protest and an appeal to bring the troops home.

This situation has presented a valuable opportunity to build a multiracial and multicultural movement opposing war and injustice. Much of the anti-war movement, however, remains segregated. The National African-American Network Against U.S. Intervention in the Gulf has been formed in part because African-American activists have felt excluded from both the National Campaign for Peace in the Middle East and the National Coalition Against U.S. Intervention in the Middle East. Segregation is reinforced by the high level of anti-war organizing occurring in the churches and the schools, two of the most segregated institutions in the country. Women have taken important leadership positions in the anti-war movement, but often remain excluded from some leadership bodies, particularly within the churches.

If the anti-war movement remains segregated, it will forfeit the opportunity to conduct a dialogue among the many communities affected by the war, and thus the opportunity to forge a united movement which speaks to the experiences of a majority of the U.S. public. Further, the anti-war movement must include the victims of injustice if it is to argue convincingly that the war is unjust.

War is Too Costly

Perhaps the single greatest difference between the movement against the war in the Gulf and previous anti-war movements is the widespread participation of active-duty and reserve military personnel, and their families. In every war, resistance within the military has been significant; during the Vietnam War it may have been decisive. The families of soldiers, as well, have always been represented in peace marches. But by all accounts, opposition among military families and outright resistance within the military is unprecedentedly high.

To some extent, this is due to the remnants of the Vietnam Syndrome: the memory of that bloody, divisive war has been stirred up by the current crisis, and this has spurred the opposition. The massive call-up of reserve forces, however, has probably been the most significant factor. Tens of thousands of reservists have been called to active duty; their lives, and their families' lives, have been disrupted. Millions of people in the United States suddenly have had to face the prospect of losing a loved one in battle. For many reservists, the reserve has been a way to get extra income, or training in a skill; their commitment to the military's objectives, and the commitment of their families, is generally lower than that of the regular forces. Young people and students have also joined the anti-war movement in significant numbers; many are worried about the possible resumption of a draft.

Soldiers and their families have been raising compelling questions: Why are we—or our loved ones—being asked to fight and die? The Bush administration's rationale keeps changing. Before the war began, numerous military experts and former secretaries of defense had called for patience; wouldn't this have been better than a bloody war? Iraq will be no pushover; thousands of U.S. soldiers will die. For what compelling national interest?

A few months after the crisis began, something approaching a national consensus had emerged: a war in the Gulf would be costly, and not worth the price in human lives. Interestingly, however, sympathy for the plight of soldiers facing war in the Saudi desert, and for the families left behind, has been generated less by the anti-war movement, which should be interested in it, than by the media. Profiles of the families of military personnel in the Gulf have appeared in countless newspapers and magazines, reaching into mainstream U.S. society in ways the peace and justice movement rarely achieves.

The anti-war movement can put a political edge on this broad popular sentiment by actively turning sympathy into solidarity. Increasingly, calls are heard at peace rallies: "Support the Troops—Bring Them Home!" Anti-war groups have given many military resisters political support, and in some cases, have provided financial and legal support as well. Family members have proven to be effective spokespersons for a movement which has the potential of truly mass support.

Cultural differences, however, have inhibited the development of close ties with the rest of the anti-war movement. Because of the racial and class composition of the military, family members are often poor and people of color, even though media attention has usually focused on the families of middle-class white soldiers. By limiting the participation of poor people and people of color, groups dominated by middle-class whites have also kept out family members of military personnel. At the same time, middle-class white military families often are politically conservative and culturally "All-American"; many of them are new to protest marches, and their flag-waving style has sometimes kept them at a distance from others in the anti-war movement.

War is Just Plain Wrong

An anti-war movement which includes Arab Americans and Jewish Americans can propose realistic alternatives to war in the Middle East, showing the public that war is unnecessary. A movement which includes poor people and people of color can make an effective argument that war is unjust. A movement which includes military personnel and their families can convince the public that a war would be too costly. A movement which includes all of these groups can create a widely-shared popular belief that war is just plain wrong. In this case, the government may win the war against Iraq, but fail to gain public support for a "new world order" based on U.S. military might and political hegemony.

It won't be easy. The Gulf crisis has deeply divided the Arab-American community, and the intensification of anti-Arab racism at home has prevented many Arab Americans from speaking out. From the beginning of the crisis, progressive Jewish-American groups have been divided between their traditional anti-war sympathies and their concern for Israel's security. Racism continues to erect barriers to multiracial and multicultural organizing.

Will Arabs, under attack in the Middle East and in the United States, feel secure enough to provide leadership for the anti-war movement? Will African Americans and Jewish Americans be able to overcome the complex tensions between their communities to make common cause against the war? Can the anti-war movement embrace both pacifists and military families, both flag-wavers and flag-burners?

If we can build a diverse movement, we might be able not only to stop the war in the Gulf. We can also create an Iraq Syndrome, a deep popular aversion to U.S. intervention which might prevent future wars in the 1990s and beyond. As we try to stop this war, let's look beyond it, and try to stop the next one, too.

Part III
Short-and Long-Term
Tasks for Peace

Encouraging Dissent
From Within

Working with
Conscientious Objectors

Michael Marsh of the War Resisters League

What are the steps people can take to help themselves or others resist the military? How does helping individual conscientious objectors and others fit into the strategy of ending war? These are the questions activists in the War Resisters League face every day. Marsh makes an impassioned argument that we must not limit our activism to arguments that are "politically palatable" but instead make the connections between helping individuals resist war and ending militarism.

Phone calls began streaming into the War Resisters League office within two weeks of Bush's decision to send troops to the region, first from the parents, friends, and lovers of those in the military, and then from those in the services themselves. Many soldiers were skeptical that the WRL could do anything about their plight. But more and more have contacted us—over 1,000 by February 1991. About 80 percent want to file for conscientious objector (CO) status as people opposed to war in any form.

Most of those who call us went into the military when they were 17 or 18 years old, straight out of high school, and are now between the ages of 21 and 23. Some are U.S. soldiers who were stationed in Germany during the Cold

War and are now facing transfer to Saudi Arabia. Many resisters are black Muslims faced with a religious dilemma—they are forbidden to kill fellow Muslims—and are opposed to fighting in this particular war. At Fort Campbell, where there are a number of Muslim soldiers, thier dilemma is ignored by the military which insists that CO status must be based on opposition to all war and does not allow for opposition to particular wars. WRL and some Islamic organizations are challenging this regulation.

Many of the soldiers who contact us have been influenced by events like the invasion of Panama and Grenada and the Iran-Contra scandal. These were events of major political significance in opening the eyes of some soldiers.

Resisters come from all branches of the military—the Army, Navy, Marine Corps, Air Force, and even the Coast Guard. We have had calls from National Guard units, active duty and reserve soldiers. To our surprise, 40 to 50 percent of the calls have been from Marines. I would have expected them to come from the Army or Navy, where drive and motivation is seen to be lower than it is in the Marine Corps. It may be a result of the Marine boot camp experience which is so harsh that many people feel brutalized by it. Rather than being beaten into submission, they have their eyes opened. They are confronted so directly by U.S. militarism that they can't help but have a different perspective of it afterwards.

Resisters in the Marine Fox Company, based at Fort Schuyler in the Bronx, illustrate what faces some of those trying to get out. Thirteen out of 150 people in this Marine company, almost 10 percent, have filed for CO or medical discharges since August. We helped several Fox Company Marines put together CO applications. One story appears in this book.

This contact with the Fox Company came after WRL and Hands Off! held a demonstration outside the base and handed out leaflets. In the following months we had numerous calls from Marines in the company. A group of

them went Unauthorized Absence (UA)—the Marine
Corps equivalent of AWOL. They were worried that reporting to base with their CO applications would result in
the military shipping them off to Saudi Arabia. Their fear
was not unfounded. Other soldiers who have filed CO
applications and have refused to deploy to the Gulf are
being put in shackles and leg irons, forced onto planes and
sent to Saudi Arabia, despite this being against Marine
Corps regulations. While they were UA, the military harassed them, sending two to four military police to their
houses, and to their parents' houses. Military watch for
their return was posted around the clock. In an attempt
to find them, the FBI interviewed the parents of the young
men. At least one phone call was interrupted by the FBI.

About a month later, under the glaring eye of the
media, they surrendered. The military treated them quite
gingerly at first, letting them go home in the evenings and
promising to process their CO applications. When the press
attention had died down two weeks later, they were shipped
down to Camp Lejeune in North Carolina, and held in
barracks. They faced physical danger from gung-ho Marines
who resented their objection to war. The camp commander
had to post military police to keep other Marines away and
told the CO Marines not to leave their barracks in groups of
less than three. No disciplinary procedures were taken
against the Marines who attacked the COs.

Choosing CO Status

The reasons for choosing conscientious objection to
war are complex. Most objections are political and
moral. Opposition to war on political grounds is ex-
pressly forbidden as a means of obtaining CO status. It
must be couched only in moral terms or the application
will be denied, despite the inseparability of morality and
politics for many.

Two political issues are racism and sexism in the

military. The military is a tremendously racist institution. One reservist in the Air Force, Haitian-born Ronald Jean-Baptiste, enlisted seeking job training. During a blood donor session at boot camp his blood was refused on the grounds that Haiti has a statistically high incidence of AIDS. Yet in New York City, the incidence of AIDS is extremely high, but blood was not refused from New Yorkers. Ronald Jean-Baptiste began to realize that the institution, of which he was now a part, was not working in his interest. He decided to resist.

Patriarchal sexism drives some women to resist. Experiencing the hierarchical structure and discrimination often reveals the nature of militarism. Resisters rarely talk about patriarchy and militarism or the connection between the two, but that is what they are describing.

Some people are resisting from a principled position of having a moral and ethical objection to war. These people choose the difficult route of being a CO. Some are resisting because of their own self-interest. They don't want to be killed. They realize, perhaps for the first time, what being in the military is really about.

Making a stand and filing for CO status is one of the hardest routes out. If you have an ulcer, or the military discovers you are gay, that will get you out a lot quicker than if you are morally opposed to war. If you are politically opposed, CO status is no way to get out at all.

One woman's story makes clear the depth of commitment by COs to taking a principled position. For reasons that will become clear, her name is withheld. When she called WRL, she began talking about the war. Her views were quite clearly that of a CO. She was morally opposed to war and to militarism. She had spent three years in the Navy. During the course of counseling, she indicated that she was a lesbian. I pointed out to her that she could get out of the service far quicker as a lesbian than as a CO. The military is extremely homophobic. They kick out gay and lesbian people as soon as they are found. She related stories of Navy witch hunts against lesbians. If a woman turns down the sexual advances of male personnel a report might be made or rumors started that the woman is a lesbian. An investigation is begun. Female friends of that woman are suspected. The witch hunt grows and grows. She had seen this happen in the Navy and kept quiet about it. I explained to her that this was the quickest way of getting out. She refused. She did not want to take part in the homophobia of the military. She did not want to take advantage of the discrimination that gay people face—it would simply reinforce the homophobia. Even if, as in this case, it was for her own good.

Recruiting Basics: Playing on Poverty, Racism, and Sexism

It is puzzling to many people why some who enlisted voluntarily are now resisting. Indeed, one journalist asserted "you went in because you wanted certain benefits from the military and now that the going is getting tough you want out." But, as with so many issues, the context of the story is not told by the media. This presentation of a CO's case ignores the poverty, racism, and sexism in society used as tools in recruiting by the military.

Eight years of the Reagan administration and two years of Bush have gutted federal financial assistance programs for college and job training. At the same time, the military recruitment budget went from $500 million to the current $2.5 billion. Recruiting techniques became more sophisticated and focused on offering job training. This is the economic draft. There was no one standing with a gun pointed at people's heads and saying "either you go in the military or you go to jail." But people were having college tuition bills ransomed: "If you want to go to college you have to go into the military."

Seventy to 80 percent of the soldiers who contact us

are African-American, almost twice the percentage they represent in the military. About 5 percent are latino. The remainder are caucasian. This distribution of large numbers of people denied access to opportunities currently available to the white middle class belies the reality of the economic and racist draft. African-American youth often see the military as their only option for getting a college education or job training. Enlistment for them may have no basis in the idealistic beliefs that the U.S. military is the champion of global democracy. It's hardly surprising, then, that people who were forced into the military for educational and economic reasons are going to be the first to want to get out, even against a backdrop of taunts by the media and physical threats from fellow soldiers.

Military recruiting is also targetting women with similar bait offered to blacks and other oppressed people. In a sexist society where opportunities for women are limited and pay is less than 70 percent of what men receive for the same work, glamorous, prestigious opportunities are dangled by military recruiters. Women can be generals or pilots. Yet women who seek these non-traditional jobs find themselves tracked into low-skill clerical positions, the nursing profession, and food services. The high-tech electronic communications positions advertised on television are not a reality for them.

The WRL Task: Counseling Resisters

After many years of peace-time work against the slick military recruiting, WRL is now faced with overwhelming requests for help. We ask callers what they think about the U.S. deployment and war in the Gulf. The retort is nearly always, "It's stupid; it doesn't make sense; this is George Bush trying to show he's tough; I don't have anything at stake here."

Unfortunately, none of these responses will get any-one out of the military. At our office or with a local counselor we hold an interview to explore their views, establish what branch they are in, their length of service and what they want from us. Most people want to explore their options. Most want to get out of the military.

There is no easy solution that will work for everyone. We build a strategy for each individual to accomplish their discharge, and a press strategy. We help them choose how political they want to be, if they want to make a statement against the armed forces. Getting a discharge as a CO or going AWOL or UA and facing the risk of one to five years in prison are difficult decisions. They need to consider dealing with the press. They risk alienating their family, friends, and fellow soldiers for their beliefs. There have been dozens of people who have decided to go the difficult route of being morally opposed to war.

WRL reviews with them the approximately twelve administrative discharges, including CO. Discharge for hardship is granted when a military person has either minors or elderly persons dependent on them. A more unusual discharge is community hardship. An example is someone in Utah who is the only doctor in a community of several thousand people. Medical discharge, and dis-charge for a variety of physical and mental conditions, including asthma, is also possible. There are also dis-charges for being gay and for fraudulent enlistment.

We are faced with the need to work with individual soldiers and the need to stop the war, which will help all soldiers. Our scarce resources are divided between outreach, training counselors, and counseling military personnel.

Our political strategy extends beyond outreach. Spending all our time leafletting and persuading people to desert, then leaving them as victims of the military justice system, would be useless; they would lose every time. We work with veterans to build an infrastructure which includes assisting soldiers after their decision to put themselves at risk. We provide them with legal assistance, community support and media coverage to help publicize their plight.

The many people coming forward to be counselors are trained to understand military enlistment policies, militarization of youth on high school campuses, and CO discharges. People don't know this information because they have been blind to the political crisis of the last ten years. Training sessions include members of churches, attorneys and people from congressional offices. We are making a military law counselor's training tape to assist people in becoming counselors. We are working with the National Lawyers Guild and CCCO and AFSC to produce a lawyer's desk book which would update and supplement the existing military law counselor's manual.

Our work in high schools to educate students about the military before they enlist is far easier than helping them get out after boot camp. We are concerned about large programs held in several thousand high schools designed to militarize young people and lure them into service. These include the Junior Reserve Officer Training Corp (JROTC) program and the "armed services vocational aptitude battery" (ASVAB), which is a military recruitment tool disguised as a vocational aptitude test.

Our efforts with high schools have met with some success. Some high schools have seen JROTC programs withdrawn because of community resistance. Schools have managed to prevent new JROTC programs from opening up and instituted broader rights for students who refuse to take the ASVAB test. Some students realize they have been duped into their military program, after hearing a veteran or a speaker from WRL, CCCO or AFSC.

The Broader Implications for Activists

This crisis has shown that the largely white, self-defined "peace movement" is not capable of handling this situation by itself. Brought together by an understanding of war as a real threat to the life of friends and relatives, rather than an abstract political occurrence, high schools and veterans' groups are working with community organizations, which have always understood that the military robs communities of resources and is sexist and racist.

Groups which normally have not worked well together are cooperating in this crisis. This hasn't happened before. It has made for some difficult meetings, especially over issues such as linkage of the crisis with Palestine. Groups like the Palestinian Solidarity Committee and WRL, who see the resolution of the Palestinian issue as integral to solving the Gulf crisis, have met with great reluctance on the part of some Jewish peace activists to make that link.

We must insist on parallels with the Vietnam War, despite Bush's desperate pleas for us to believe that there are none. Both wars are immoral. In each case, there is economic exploitation of a region and of a people. African Americans and Latinos died at higher rates during the Vietnam War than would have been expected, given their numbers in the U.S. population. Given the similar make-up of the force today, that is likely to recur.

One of the peace movement's weaknesses is that we are totally unable to deal with quick U.S. military strikes. We were completely ineffective at preventing the invasion of Panama and Grenada. They caught some of us totally by surprise. Those who were prepared could not get anyone else to listen to them soon enough to take action to stop the invasion. In the future we need to do more to insure our readiness to protest quick U.S. military actions. There are a lot of small countries that the United States may strike, which makes developing this response capacity important.

From Counseling Individuals to Ending Militarism

Helping people file for CO status may be all for the good, but, one might well ask, how does helping these individuals contribute to ending war? To answer this question, we must look at the nature of militarism.

Boys are trained as warriors in our society. They learn that in order to be men they have to act aggressively, be competitive, and treat women in a dominating way. They can prove their manhood by going into the military. This is especially true of many of the Marines who have come to our office. They were attracted by the uniform, the bulging muscles and brass buttons of the recruitment posters. They wanted to be "one of the proud." Parents need to understand that the sort of toys they buy for their children will influence the sort of adults they become. GI Joe dolls and pushing them to excel in wrestling, boxing, football, etc., will groom their sons as Marines. Playing with Barbie dolls and saying "yes" to boys will make compliant women out of daughters.

In helping people get out of the military and resisting war, we begin unlearning militarism. But we also have to take a longer-term vision, to address racism, sexism, economic exploitation and U.S. nationalism, hegemony and imperialism. If Americans are only able to stand up and cry out against wars in which their son or daughter might die and not against all the other U.S.-funded wars around the world, then we are only doing half our job. We need to bring in longer-term political objectives and not be afraid to alienate people as we enlighten and educate them. Some people are going to be alienated and turn us off before they give us a second glance. We need to take that risk. We cannot be strapped by only using arguments that are politically palatable while avoiding the real causes for this crisis: U.S. economic exploitation and long-term military domination of the Middle East.

Refusing to Participate in Interventionist Wars

U.S. Marine Corporal Erik Larsen

Is refusal to go to war by those in the armed forces based on self-interest? As Larsen exemplifies, the analysis driving many to resist makes connections between the Persian Gulf crisis, militarism, and domestic issues. The motivation for many is a deep sense that justice—not the orders of the commander-in-chief—must be served.

On April 21, 1986, I joined the Marine Corps to defend the American dream, which first attracted my parents to this country in 1958. I emerged from boot camp three months later, a fully indoctrinated fighting machine willing to go anywhere in the world to defend the ideals and freedoms stated in the Constitution of the United States of America.

I am now a Lance Corporal in the U.S. Marine Corps Reserve and a radar mechanic for the HAWK missile system. I am stationed in Hayward, California at the Fourth Light Anti-Aircraft Missile Battalion, Fourth Marine Aircraft Wing.

I first became aware of the realities of U.S. policies through student activists at Chabot Community College in California. They introduced me to alternative newspapers and books, and exposed me to the writings and speeches of Archbishop Oscar Romero of El Salvador. I learned about the Central American history of U.S.-sponsored exploitative policies motivated by corporate and personal greed. Seventy thousand Salvadorans have been killed over the last ten years as a result of U.S. policies. I realized I could no longer blindly follow orders from my commander-in-chief but that my actions were ultimately accountable to a higher authority—namely God.

My deeply-rooted moral convictions have led me to declare my objections to the escalation of tensions and seemingly inevitable war in the Middle East.

It sickens me to hear Mr. Bush announce that several hundred thousand of my reservist and active duty brothers and sisters are going to wage war in the Middle East to protect "our American lifestyle." Oil imports could be cut in half if a sound energy policy focusing on renewable resources and conservation was in effect. Our oil-consuming western lifestyle is destroying the earth, and it is our wasteful society that has brought the world to the brink of a preventable war.

Our presence in the Middle East has destroyed any hope of any of us ever receiving a peace dividend. We are wasting more than $24 million a day in Saudi Arabia while the schools are in shambles, homeless people still walk the streets, and the S&L criminals are still on the loose.

I've been listening to a lot of experts on television and radio and they share my concern that the use of chemical and tactical nuclear weapons is a possibility in the event war does occur. I have experienced firsthand the frightening power of chemical weapons, and I never want to go through that again. I had two buddies who were involved in a chemical incident when I was on an exercise at Dugway Proving Grounds in Utah. They were rushed to an aid station while a decontamination team swept the area.

The suggestion that nuclear weapons could be used in addition to chemical weapons scares the hell out of me. The use of chemical-biological agents and nuclear arms is completely unjustified. Eight years ago, the Reagan-Bush administration encouraged the sale of chemical weapons to Saddam Hussein. Bush said nothing at the time about human rights when Saddam used the weapons on his own people. Bush wants us to forget that he turned his eyes when innocent men, women and children were being gassed.

Now he wants the American public to turn our eyes and forget about humanity, as he prepares to use me and others in the service as fodder for his cannon. I spent three long months in boot camp to learn to view human beings as targets. It has taken me almost three years to begin to see people as individiuals once again. And I'll be damned if I'm going to be a part of this militaristic feeding frenzy.

The only settlement of this crisis is the complete withdrawal of all forces from the area and the start of honest negotiations. I hope to God that it won't take a row of body bags to finally wake people up. I hope that my refusal to support this war may in someway help end U.S. intervention in the Middle East.

I will refuse orders to activate me into the regular Marines.

I will refuse orders to ship me to Saudi Arabia to defend our polluting exploitative lifestyle.

I will refuse to face another human being with a gas mask covering my face and my M-16 drawn.

I declare myself a conscientious objector. I am no longer a Marine.

The Fox Company,
not the Box Company

Sam Lwin

*What is the journey traveled by someone who joins
the military to make something of himself and later files
for conscientious objector status? Sam Lwin provides the
unique perspective of an immigrant making those choices,
taken in by the high ideals which drape American political
life, only to find himself resisting the principle of war
lurking behind the rhetoric. Using the slogan, "The Fox
Company, not the Box Company," he and several other
Marines in the Fox Company organized a campaign to
prevent his company from going to war.*

*By what right can a soldier disobey orders? Stormin'
Norman—as General Norman Schwarzkopf, commander
of the forces in the war against Iraq, likes to be called—
made his position clear in a recent interview as he reflected
on his role in the invasion of Grenada. "Grenada. I asked
myself why on earth the U.S. was getting involved in
Grenada. Then I said, Schwarzkopf, just let it sort itself
out. You're an instrument of policy. You don't make policy."
This reasoning is similar to that used by Nazis at the
Nuremberg trials—they were just following orders. Lwin
rejects this, clear that he must obey the principles set out
at Nuremberg, and refuse to go to war.*

Coming to the United States

I never knew my parents. I never knew if I had any
brothers or sisters or anyone who was genetically bonded
to me. I grew up in Burma with a family that had eight

kids and a "dad" and a "mom." I'm not sure at what age I started to hang out with them. They sent me to school where I learned to add and subtract and things like that. The teachers were mean and strict. If you talked to anyone in class you'd get hit; if you did things you weren't supposed to do, you'd get hit; and if you didn't do things you were supposed to do, you'd get hit. I got sick of it because I was always at the end of that stick. I usually greased myself before going to school. There was never a day I didn't get into trouble. At the age of eight I came to America to live with a family who were relatives of the family in Burma. For a while I lived with them, but things didn't work out, so I left them when I was 16. I went to live with my neighbor who became my guardian.

College and the Marines

I attended college in the fall of 1987. I didn't have much time to study because I was working nearly full-time. I enlisted in the Marines in February 1988. There are many reasons why I joined the Marine Corps. My ex-roommate was in the Coast Guard and I thought he was doing something with his life. When he came home from drill I saw him in his uniform and felt I wanted to be an American too.

I felt that America was a good country, that the government was good, that it helps out other people, other countries. That's what I thought at the time. I thought it was a democracy and I wanted to uphold that democracy. "Serve your country." I was taken in by the rhetoric.

Being independent most of my life, I was attracted to what the recruiting officer offered: a chance to go places, assistance for college, some medical and dental benefits, life insurance, and especially, a skill which could later help me to get further in life. The military gives you this propaganda line, that you'll get a very good job after you leave the military, that you'll get a good skill and all kinds of benefits. I was working full-time and going to school full-time and I needed some money. But later on I found out I didn't need it that bad.

At the time I enlisted, on February 9, 1988, I was unsure of what I wanted from life. I knew I wanted to be a part of something and thought I could be part of "the Few and the Proud." And I thought maybe the military was something about which I could later say, "I am proud of going through this experience." In some ways I did look at the Marines as a challenge in reaching my adulthood. The Marines were into "shaping character," things like that. That's the reason why I joined. And in part, I thought that enemies are wicked, evil people.

When I was sworn in, in front of an officer, I did not object to killing an enemy in war or dying for this country. Remembering Adolf Hitler and the Nazi regime, I felt that an enemy is a creature of total evil and that it deserves nothing less than a severe punishment and death. At that time, I did not think that an enemy is a human being like myself—that he is capable of loving, understanding, feeling, and attaining all human virtues. I was still ignorant of reality.

My moral and philosophical principles were still in an uncrystallized form. Since coming to America I hadn't attended Buddhist temples as frequently as I did in Burma. I was too busy being assimilated into American culture. Yet I have always treasured my childhood teachings about being kind and bringing happiness to others. I did and do see human life as something precious, but I still could not articulate it. I remember standing in front of my history class in high school and trying to explain why we should not have the death penalty. I did say that life is too precious to be wasted and that hardened criminals may see the light in prison. Aside from those two sentences I felt stupid; I couldn't go on any further.

Boot Camp

On May 24, 1988 I went to boot camp at Parris Island. The day I got off the bus, there was a big guy screaming, yelling, trying to belittle us. He was supposed to be "the man," supposed to tell us what to do, treat us like, you might even say, slaves. Ever since the first day we came off that bus we were being herded into one place and drilled. They give you certain rules and laws, and they keep instilling fear. Like if you violate Article 86 (Unauthorized Absence), you can get in a lot of trouble, only they say it in a more frightening way. They say if you strike an officer you're gonna get it. If you do this, you're gonna get it, do that, you're gonna get it. Whatever you do, you'll always be watched, wherever you go.

When the daily trumpet comes on, I'm supposed to stand, I'm supposed to look at the flag, I'm supposed to do this, act this way, eat this way, march and talk this way. I realized there was no chance even to think. There's no such thing as individuality. We're supposed to obey all orders immediately without any questioning whatsoever. That's what discipline was. You have to act this way because there's always somebody watching you. That was one of the main impressions I got. The treatment was deliberately dehumanizing. We're being shaped, broken down. All our individuality, whatever civilian past life we had, was erased, eradicated.

It was in this wasteland of boot camp that I began to understand the true meaning of compassion for humanity and the value of life itself. I and my fellow recruits were treated like machines. We were taught to march and act like one; we ate, slept, and woke up like one. We were screamed at, yelled at, and laughed at, as though we weren't human beings capable of feeling and understanding. Our names were associated with numbers and things. We were drilled into instant obedience to all orders and respect for authority.

After weeks of experiencing this daily, I began to resist the training process. I became a "run-drop" in physical training. When no one was looking while I marched alone in the forest, I started to walk like a normal person. I tried my best to stay away from my platoon as much as possible by going to sickbay under all kinds of excuses. I tried my best to fail swimming qualification so that I wouldn't have to see much of my drill sergeants. I was always the last one to finish meals. I also did many other things that I was not supposed to do and got into all sorts of trouble for them. Finally, my drill sergeants got sick of me and put me on trial training.

During rifle training I found I did not like shooting. I knew it was a weapon for destructive purposes. I had anxiety attacks whenever it was my turn to shoot. This led me to fail the rifle examination.

At sickbay and at training I met recruits who had tried to commit suicide and had done things to get out of Parris Island. I could not blame them; this whole training cycle was a dehumanizing process and the only way to recover their sanity was to do what they did. I felt bad for them. Somehow, I wished that I had done the same.

For many months after boot camp I tried to put my past behind me, but found that I could not. My whole daily routine was changed drastically: I was always late for work, late for school, and late for everything. I slept twelve hours a day and sometimes forgot to eat. I was always forgetting things and finally I had to look into myself and see what was wrong with me. I still have nightmares about the military.

Strengthening Values and Learning More About War

During the last two years several books and movies strengthened my moral and religious beliefs. Works by

Dostoyevsky including *Crime and Punishment, The Idiot, The Brothers Karamazov,* and *The Underground Man* helped me formulate and solidify my beliefs about the value of human life. In the *Autobiography of Malcolm X,* I was able to see the struggle of one person's determination to fight for social justice and the value of humility, respect, and brotherhood.

War movies like *The Goodfellas,* and others gave me a full picture of the insanity of violence. I was very disgusted to see bodies dismembered and hanged; it was very dehumanizing even in fiction. Movies like *Darkman, Last Temptation of Christ,* and *Ghost* made me see the man inside and not the man in the physical and the material. Films like *Platoon* and *Full Metal Jacket* helped me, in part, to conclude that war is not a solution to conflict. The scenes in *El Salvador* and posters of corpses in my school shocked me beyond belief. It angered me to hear about the deaths of so many students and working people at the hands of the military, like in Beijing, Burma, and in parts of Europe.

Since the Gulf Crisis Began

When Bush mobilized the first wave of troops to Saudi Arabia, it didn't really seem to have much to do with me because I was in the Reserves and they might not call up the Reserves. But late in September I realized that there might be a big war and a lot of people could start dying. Late in September I was put on alert. The word was out: any day they could call us up and we should be prepared.

I knew I didn't want to be part of a war. So I went to the War Resisters League and found out about conscientious objector status. Although I had heard about conscientious objection in my freshman year of college, I had thought you had to be a total pacifist, and I, for one, am not. I cannot stand by and watch injustice done to anyone.

After reading the material they gave me at the War Resisters League I realized that I do qualify for conscientious objection.

I spent a month writing the essays for my conscientious objector application. Filing a CO claim makes you think carefully about your beliefs. Finally, on November 9 I went to hand in my CO application to my commanding officer. I had a showdown with the captain and he blew up. He waged a psychological war on me, but couldn't persuade me to change my mind. He said things like, "when you're walking down the street one day, I hope a mugger stabs you," or "I hope the sergeants and other non-commissioned officers beat the shit out of you when they find out you applied for conscientious objection." I told him, "I don't care if the general beats the shit out of me, I'm going to do everything in my power to defend myself." He asked me why I suddenly changed my mind, and I said that my mind changed in boot camp and these two years helped me see the reality. He asked me if I still take the GI Bill and checks and I said they're filthy and I'd rather give everything back. He said, "I know you're lying to me." What is this bullshit? Can't a guy disagree and refuse to commit mass murder against the people of Iraq and third world nations? I'm sorry if the captain is pissed off. I'd hate to see him fragged [murdered by subordinate soldiers] if this turns out to be a long war and the troops get sick of it.

In this day and age, I still can't believe our generation of people would rather solve problems by blowing each other's brains out. What the hell is wrong with people? Are we so brainwashed that we still listen to those insane people in the government? We know this is for oil, and we know every war waged throughout the centuries has been for expansion of wealth, land, and power. We know it's always the poor people, and people in general, going to kill for rich corporations like Exxon and Texaco. Why do we keep listening to the few? We don't need those troops in Saudi Arabia to bring home more racism, sexism, ignorance, homelessness, apathy, antipathy, violence, and homophobia. We've already had enough from past wars. I'm sick of it.

I'm sorry if Bush thinks and feels Saddam Hussein is another Hitler. They used to be good buddies a few months back before the invasion of Kuwait. Many of the weapons Hussein has were sold to him by our government. Now Bush is willing to have many die at the hands of weapons sold to Iraq.

Organizing Conscientious Objectors and other Anti-War Actions

I was not very political before all this started. But becoming a conscientious objector has made it necessary for me to speak out. In addition to speaking at several rallies and in defense of two people who tried to stop the outbreak of war against Iraq and are being tried on ridiculous charges, I joined the War Resisters League. I helped found a student organization called Hands Off!, supporting resisters in New York and all over the country.

I always thought a lot of people out there don't really care about other people. I found out that's not true. There are a lot of people who are willing to organize, who care about justice.

Resisting War and Personal Change

As a result of my strengthened moral and philosophical beliefs, and my notion of brotherhood and sisterhood, I find myself treating others with more kindness and respect than in the past. I can see now the pain faced by beggars and homeless people who deserve our respect and help. I give them money and food, and sympathize with them. Many of my friends and classmates are starting to realize some changes in me. I now go to Buddhist temples more often than I have in the past twelve years, and have developed stronger moral, social, philosophical, and religious feelings. Money and material desire are becoming less important to me. My compassion for everyone, even criminals and enemies, has reached a higher stage.

I also find myself more in contact with the world. I read newspapers daily and write to my friends whenever I can. I am not as socially withdrawn as I used to be.

From a starting point that war is wrong, my political activism is broadening to encompass other issues and their relationship to each other. I do believe in freedom, democracy, and equality for humankind, but I want to pursue it through nonviolent means. I am planning to become an activist in the struggle to make homes for homeless people, to create jobs for the unemployed, to strengthen our children's education, to fight racism, sexism, and many other unjust things in society.

Links between many issues are clear. The government doesn't really care about the people in this country. Look at Vietnam Vets. Many are homeless. Twenty, thirty years ago they went to fight for this country and when they came back the government didn't really care about them. They are homeless. A lot of them committed suicide. A lot of them did a lot of drugs and alcohol. Some of them, even if they're still living physically, they're dead already. You can see it in their faces. They're not there any more. Their human aspect is gone. All you see is a sad person who lost himself.

We are living on centuries of lies. We must dig up our past and see the truths for ourselves. A revolution must take place—a revolution in our minds, hearts, and souls. We must break away from our present thinking and feeling and consciousness. We have been conditioned by the media and what past generations of brainwashed forefathers have told us. We must fight for this freedom. Ignorance and hatred will be our hardest foes. We must

wake up our long-lost sisters and brothers. It's the powerful who have kept us ignorant, separate, and apart.

If I hadn't joined the military and learned what it's
all about, and they had called me up to war in a draft, I
probably would have gone. If I hadn't been part of the
Marines I might not have had this awakening. It was in
the Marines I realized I was being used for something, for
some purpose, and it was probably by rich people who
have power. I was being used as "a pawn in the struggle
for American international power," as Eric Hayes, another Marine conscientious objector said. I saw how the
military had treated my life, and the lives of others: as
though they are worth nothing.

It's a fight on behalf of rich people and for the
government. It's a plutocracy. Many in the military are
really poor. A lot of them are blacks and hispanics forced
into the military because of this racist economic system.
The poor and oppressed are going off to fight for the rich
and the powerful. How many congresspersons' sons and
daughters have anything to do with war? Will Neil Bush
ever go to war? If there is a draft, the rich will pull some
strings with government agencies to pay their way out of
going to war. It's sick.

In learning about the United States, I realized that
the government funds death squads in El Salvador. When
the U.S. invaded Panama, killing so many Panamanian
civilians, like many others I was ignorant. It's difficult to
break out of that ignorance. The newspapers and television news show troops saying "yeah, we went in, we did
it, we did the job, this is America, we're being patriotic."
But they don't show you the other side. A lot of soldiers
killed civilians indiscriminately for the hell of it. They
didn't show that. They didn't show "friendly fire"—soldiers accidently killing one another off. The news picture
is unquestioning.

We must redefine patriotism, from blowing some
guy's brain out just because the government tells you he's

your enemy, to upholding the ideals of democracy. It must mean helping the people of this country; to help create peace and prevent war. That's what patriotism is.

Even from the start I knew I might not get this status. I feel it. That was partly the reason why I went public, as well as to let other people know this status is available. I have a very strong argument, a very strong claim. But if the Pentagon says your claim is political in nature, you won't get it. For the Pentagon to deny my status would reveal a lot of hypocrisy. Lately, I've been hearing rumors that they may court-martial me. But I don't care if I end up in jail for ten years or so; I'm not going to splatter people's guts and brains with an M-16. I'd rather die than murder any of my brothers and sisters.

Recently, I heard that five guys in North Carolina refused to go to Saudi Arabia and sat down on the airstrip. The commanding officer had them in handcuffs and chains on their legs and put them on a plane to Saudi Arabia. That's totally immoral. How can we talk about democracy when the military itself is not a democracy? Two years ago, part of the reason I joined was to uphold democracy. I believed in America, the government and everything. But now I realize the military is not a democracy, and that there is a great deal to change if we are to make America live up to the ideals it holds.

After World War II, when Japanese and German soldiers were convicted of war crimes, their argument was that they were just following orders. And that's what the government is telling me to do now, to just follow orders. Back in the 1940s, this government upheld the Nuremberg Principle, that every soldier has a moral responsibility for his actions. I believe in the Nuremberg Principle. We must question the authorities and stand up for our beliefs, even if it means going to prison.

Reclaiming Democracy

Congress and the Creation of a Just Middle East Policy

Nancy Murray
and Hady Amr

*What is the policy we would prefer the United States
to pursue in the Middle East? What steps could we take to
implement it? Murray makes a definitive case for a policy
which includes linkage and resolution of the Palestinian
question, and strategies to force Congress to implement it.*

The Bush administration's maneuvers have brought
the devastation of war. Instead of seeking solutions
through negotiations, the administration has been using
diplomacy to battle ghosts and keep possible solutions at
bay.

The Question of Linkage

Ever since Iraqi President Saddam Hussein's August 12 offer to withdraw from Kuwait if Israel would
withdraw from the lands it conquered in 1967 and Syria
and Israel would withdraw from Lebanon, this "linkage"
of the region's occupations has been a specter haunting
Bush's Gulf policy. Why has the administration been so
swift to put the lives of hundreds of thousands of U.S.
servicemen and women in jeopardy after Iraq invaded
Kuwait, while we make allies with another Middle East
occupier, Syria, and we refuse to use the $11 million per

163

day we give in grants to Israel as leverage over its twenty-three-year-long occupation of the Palestinian West Bank, Gaza and East Jerusalem?

We have concocted an "international consensus" for the use of force against Iraq, by steering clear of the UN General Assembly and instead cajoling the handful of nations in the Security Council into shortcircuiting the time given for sanctions to work, thereby violating the UN Charter which states that force can only be a measure of last resort. Meanwhile, we stand alone in the international community in refusing to pressure Israel to accept the principle that the acquisition of territory by force is illegitimate and that it should return the territories it captured in 1967 in exchange for peace.

The United States has gone to war in order to keep intact its record of double standards in the region. The Bush administration had little trouble making the case that Saddam Hussein's offer of August 12 was a delaying tactic, pointing out that if the solution of one problem depended on the solution of another, Iraq would be in Kuwait forever. But subsequent variations on the "linkage" theme put forward by Jordan's King Hussein, Britain, France, and the Soviet Union seemed to promise a way out of the Gulf crisis which could also lead to a resolution of the region's most intractable problems. As an editorial in the *Manchester Guardian Weekly* (UK) stated on December 9, "although 'linkage' may be ritually denied by the Bush administration, the problems of this region from Gaza to Baghdad are, in the end, indivisible."

By this time, Saddam Hussein reportedly had become more flexible in how he perceived linkage, and no longer insisted that the Israeli and Iraqi occupations had to be ended simultaneously. Former Prime Minister Edward Heath, among others, felt this was a promising development for diplomacy. On November 11, 1990, Heath spoke on British television about his meeting with Saddam Hussein: "When talking he did not directly link

the Palestine question or Israel with the question of
Kuwait and the future there... He said it was nearly
linked. Now this is very important too because it is possible therefore for the President or the Prime Minister and
others to say 'right, we are going to do this about Palestine
and for the Israelis' but without linking directly to what
is required in Kuwait... But there has got to be an exchange of views." The United States managed to ignore
this possible opening for negotiations.

A month later, as the UN Security Council debated
how to extend Palestinians international protection in the
aftermath of the October 8 Haram Al-Sharif killing of 17
Palestinians in Jerusalem and Israel's cold-shouldering of
two Security Council resolutions critical of the massacre,
there was a report that the Iraqi ambassador to Brussels
had told Jaak Gabriels, president of one of the parties in
Belgium's coalition government, that Iraq would immediately pull out of Kuwait if the United States publicly called
for the implementation of all UN resolutions on the Middle East.[1] The Iraqi ambassador also claimed that Iraq
was ready to dismantle its weapons—nuclear, chemical,
bacteriological and conventional—if other countries in the
region, including Israel, did the same.

Was there something here worth talking about? Not
as far as the Bush administration was concerned. In
mid-December it was still struggling to banish the specter
of linkage from the UN Security Council, and was not
about to make a show of support for UN resolutions
critical of the Israeli occupation. In striking contrast to
the dispatch with which the United States insisted the
Security Council act against Iraq, for almost seven weeks
it forced votes to be postponed and draft resolutions to be
rewritten in a furious bout of diplomacy designed not to
find a way of averting the war facing the anti-Iraq coalition, but to keep both its pro-Israel foreign policy and the
coalition from falling apart.

No "Reward" for Saddam Hussein

In the debates of November and December, U.S. negotiators had four primary goals: to prevent the Security Council from playing a meaningful role in overseeing the Israeli occupation; to avoid any reference in a binding resolution to a future international peace conference, on the grounds that Saddam Hussein might regard this as a "victory"; to evade any specific mention of Jerusalem as part of the occupied territories; and to avoid using its veto. By mid-December, there were signs that Washington's attempt to protect Israel on the pretext that anything else might be seen as a "reward" for Saddam Hussein was straining the anti-Iraq coalition. The Egyptian and Syrian press denounced U.S. stalling tactics. The Kuwait government-in-exile and Saudi Arabian cabinet issued statements condemning the United States for its double standard, and the European Community at its Rome summit announced in exasperation that it would break ranks with the United States on the issue of an international peace conference, and vote in favor of it even if the United States opposed it.

Within days, after Israel had announced that it was resuming its policy of expulsions in direct violation of the Fourth Geneva Convention, the United States had settled for the best deal it could get. Resolution 681 made no mention of sending a UN ombudsman to the territories, which the United States had opposed as involving the Security Council too directly in the Israeli occupation, but did support the Secretary-General's suggestion that the signatories of the 1949 Geneva Convention be convened to consider the issue of protection. The United States lost on the issue of Jerusalem, specified as part of the occupied territories. It won on the issue of an international peace conference. The notion of holding a "properly structured" conference at some "appropriate time" was relegated to a non-binding separate statement that ended with the words: "In the view of the members of the Council, the Arab-Israeli conflict is important and unique and must be addressed independently, on its own merits." Most importantly, the issue of linkage had been faced down—and the war was still on.

What is going on here? Why has avoiding any recognition that the region's problems should be seen in their totality been made to seem such an important part of our national interest—something worth dying for?

These are questions which have not been addressed in any fundamental way in the U.S. media. Neither have they figured prominently in the deliberations of the many organizations now opposing war in the Gulf. And this is a serious shortcoming.

The U.S. peace movement has long deemed the Middle East off-limits to avoid the "contentious issue" of Israel. Now we have a duty to make up for lost time, and take stock of U.S. foreign policy in the region as a whole. We must evolve strategies to avoid a war in the Middle East which will be far more effective in the long run than the simple demand that our troops come home. "U.S. troops out of the Gulf" is a necessary component of any peaceful resolution of the crisis, but is it a sufficient one? Would it by itself usher in a lasting peace to the region, or merely put the anticipated war on hold?

Only by a frank examination of all aspects of U.S. policy in the region can we comprehend how our alliance with Israel—which is unprecedented in its scope and price tag— has made the Middle East so explosive, and the extent of our own power in defusing the regional powder keg. For the Bush administration does not make Middle East policy in a vacuum. Our elected representatives play a crucial role in sustaining the relationship with Israel and shielding it from critical appraisal. We can, if we choose, exert pressure on our representatives to adopt freshness of thought and independence of action on Middle East problems, especially on those problems for which the United States is uniquely responsible.

Our Unique Alliance

Bringing such popular influence to bear on Congress is long overdue. Twenty-one years ago, Alfred Lilienthal was shocked by a vociferously pro-Israel and anti-United Nations advertisement sponsored by the American Israel Public Affairs Committee (AIPAC) in the *New York Times* to celebrate Israel's twenty-first birthday. It was signed by 59 senators and 238 representatives. It was strange, Lilienthal reported, to see 297 legislators lending their names "in support of a document drafted in the interests of a foreign country." [2]

In the years that followed, this sort of public demonstration of support for Israel became routine. The combination of political intimidation, financial encouragement and fears of Soviet expansion in the Middle East made members of Congress behave, in Lilienthal's words, "as if they were members of the Knesset." [3]

The pro-Israel groups which make up the "Israel lobby"—including AIPAC, which mobilizes pressure, 121 pro-Israel PACs with inscrutable names like Americans for Good Government and the National Action Committee, which provide cooperative congresspeople with funds and target the uncooperative for electoral defeat, various Pentagon interests and influential Christian fundamentalist organizations of the radical right—have succeeded in promoting their agenda because for the most part it has coincided with the official government position. In keeping with the Cold War mindset, it was said that Israel was a barrier to Soviet penetration of the region—a view which was doggedly maintained despite evidence that American support for Israel had considerably enhanced Soviet influence among Arab nations.

From the Arab perspective, Israel, backed by America, was responsible for the instability plaguing the region. Israel had initiated four of the seven major regional conflicts—that of 1956, 1967, the first invasion of Lebanon in 1978 and the war against Lebanon in 1982, which resulted in at least 20,000 civilian deaths. Furthermore, Israel had showed no real interest in making peace with its neighbors. Instead, since 1967 it spurned peace overtures made by Arab states and conducted incessant air strikes, described as "pre-emptive" and "retaliatory," against neighboring countries.[4] As Cheryl Rubenberg points out, the number of Arab civilians killed in one Israeli bombing raid on Beirut on July 17-18, 1981 was greater than the total number of 282 Israeli civilians killed in all acts of terrorism from 1967 to 1982.[5]

Neighboring Arab countries had ample reason to believe that Israel was more interested in expanding at their expense than in coexistence. The rhetoric of the Israeli leadership through the years and across the political spectrum, as well as the record of Israeli aggression, stoked those fears. For instance, after the Six Day War Moshe Dayan made territorial aggression fundamental to Zionism's past and future project: "During the last hundred years our people have been in a process of building up the country and the nation, of expansion, of getting additional Jews and additional settlements in order to expand the borders here. Let no Jew say the process has ended. Let no Jew say that we are near the end of the road."[6] Yitzhak Shamir could not have put it better.

While Moshe Dayan urged his countrymen to expand Israel's borders, President Nixon and National Security Adviser and later Secretary of State Henry Kissinger saw in Israel a regional surrogate—or "strategic asset"—to expand American power. Public disenchantment with the Vietnam War by the end of the 1960s was making direct American intervention anywhere in the world politically risky. But Israel, together with the Shah's Iran, could police the region in U.S. interests and act against any manifestation of Arab nationalism which threatened western domination of the region's oil resources.

In return, American economic and military aid to

Israel steadily grew. Already representing the highest per capita aid from the U.S. to any country, aid to Israel increased ninefold in the single year of 1970-71 and then continued to leap upwards. It was some eight times higher in the period 1974-1979 than in the previous six-year period, with an astonishing threefold increase occuring in 1979 as a reward for Israel's signing the Camp David accords with Egypt.

The Camp David accords, which sidestepped the Israeli-Palestinian conflict, revealed the limitations of dealing with regional issues on a piecemeal basis instead of pressing for a comprehensive solution. Egypt, which had been the most influential and militarily strongest Arab nation, was now neutralized in the American camp, giving Israel a virtual free hand to bomb and then invade Lebanon. Far from ushering in peace, Camp David intensified regional instability and created a power vacuum in the Arab world into which Saddam Hussein soon aspired to move.

Egypt's President Sadat had hoped to include in the accords a written undertaking by Israel to end its program of building settlements on occupied Palestinian lands. But Israeli Prime Minister Begin refused to have such a stipulation in the accords, leaving President Carter to give his personal guarantee that new Israeli settlements would not be undertaken. A day after the accords were signed, Israel announced a new settlement program, demonstrating that its expansionist vision had not been laid to rest.

In the decade that followed, the United States gave uncritical support to Israel as it set aside 60 percent of the Palestinian West Bank and 40 percent of the Gaza Strip for exclusive Jewish use, appropriated over 80 percent of Palestinian water resources and subjected Palestinian residents to a range of collective punishments and human rights abuses forbidden by the Fourth Geneva Convention. In opposition to U.S. policy, Israel insisted that the Fourth Geneva Convention did not apply to its role as

occupier, and simply ignored UN Security Resolutions 242
and 338 calling for its withdrawal from the occupied
territories. As promised in secret memoranda which were
a prelude to the Camp David accords, the United States
repeatedly voted against Security Council resolutions un-
favorable to Israel.

Israel was also sustained in its defiance of international law by U.S. assistance, which increased by more
than $500 million in 1983, despite its invasion of Lebanon
and indiscriminate bombing of civilians. By 1984, U.S. aid
had reached more than $2 billion per year, all of it in
grants, and is nearly double that today—a full quarter of
all our foreign assistance.

In return, the U.S. government has received a variety of covert and overt services from our "strategic ally,"
which has become much more than a regional surrogate
for American power. Under Reagan, Israel increasingly
acted as our global gendarme—undermining third world
liberation movements around the world, arming regimes
which the United States could not openly support, sharing
intelligence, testing weapons and "anti-subversion" techniques on the surrounding Arab populations, and helping
subvert the U.S. Constitution in what became known as
the "Iran-Contra scandal." [7]

The Two Branches Collide

For the most part, the executive and legislative
branches of the U.S. government have shared a common
outlook on the Middle East and on the question of U.S.
support for Israel, no matter what its consequences in
forcing embittered Arab states to turn to Moscow for
assistance and in destabilizing the region. For the most
part—but not always. On several occasions Congress,
through the political pressure it could exert and its control
of the purse, has aborted arms sales to Arab countries
which various administrations wanted to undertake. Con-

gress also has shielded Israel from presidential attempts
to pressure it to enter peace negotiations with the Palestinians.

Paul Findley, a congressperson for 22 years until the
pro-Israel lobby organized to defeat him, documents in his
book, *They Dare to Speak Out,* several examples of the way
Congress has tied the hands of the administration in its
Middle East policy. For instance, in 1975, when President
Gerald Ford wanted to "reappraise" Middle East policy
and reconsider its aid to Israel to force it to be more
cooperative, three-quarters of the Senate sent him a letter
urging a recommitment to Israel's security and a continuation of military and economic support. According to
Findley, this letter represented such a political threat that
Ford backed down and never again took on the lobby.[8]

Three years later, President Carter dealt the pro-Israel lobby one of its very few defeats when he managed,
in the face of tremendous public relations pressure (which
included flooding Capitol Hill with copies of a book about
the Holocaust) to marshall congressional support for a
sale of F-15 fighter planes to Saudi Arabia. But "Carter
was so bruised that he never again forced a showdown
vote in Congress over Middle East policy."[9]

This history should be taken into account when
assessing the performance of the Bush administration
during the recent Security Council debates over the question of "linkage." The administration had already heard
from Congress on the matter and was well aware of
political constraints on its conduct of U.S. foreign policy.
In early October, following President Bush's statement
before the UN General Assembly that a settlement of the
Israeli-Palestinian conflict could follow the withdrawal of
Saddam Hussein from Kuwait, Representatives Mel Levine (D-CA) and Charles Schumer (D-NY) launched a resolution urging the president "to keep the resolution of the
Iraqi-Kuwaiti crisis separate from any other conflict in
the region." H.Con.Res. 382 passed by a vote of 406-4. In

the Senate, Charles Grassley (R-IA) and Frank Lautenberg (D-NJ) and 51 of their colleagues sent Bush a letter voicing similar sentiments. In Grassley's view, the only instance of linkage in the Middle East was that Kuwait and Israel were both "innocent victims of attack"—a statement which went unchallenged by his colleagues, despite the fact that Israel initiated the 1967 war with a surprise attack on Egypt.

Two months later, on December 6, there was a public furor in the United States and Israel over reports that the U.S. ambassador to the U.N., Thomas Pickering, had himself introduced the idea of including an international peace conference in the UN resolution on Israel. According to a Reuters dispatch, the outcry had "poisoned the atmosphere" and the administration immediately had second thoughts.

The administration's near lapse from the politically orthodox line of what was good for Israel again stirred Congress into action. On December 10, Representatives Levine and Schumer circulated a letter addressed to Baker which demanded a U.S. veto of any Security Council resolution critical of Israel, whether or not it called for an international peace conference: "Inevitably, any UN resolution on the Palestine question at this time will implicitly be linked with the Iraqi invasion of Kuwait. This is clearly one of the aims of Saddam Hussein. To permit the passage of such a resolution now would only reward Saddam Hussein's aggression."

Congress seemed in full accord with Yitzhak Shamir, who warned during his visit to New York that Israel would not allow any solution that would appease Saddam Hussein at its expense. Coming from a nation which possesses nuclear as well as chemical weapons and is reportedly disturbed by the Arab company the United States is keeping in the anti-Iraq coalition, this is no idle threat.

Do Israel and the United States share the same aims in the Gulf crisis? According to Yosef Goell, writing in the

October 17 *Jerusalem Post,* a solution which left Iraq intact would be, for Israel "the worst of all possible outcomes." A solution which forced Israel to the negotiating table with Palestinians would be equally unpalatable to Prime Minister Shamir, who stated again on November 18, 1990 that Israel would never give up the territories it occupied.

But our Arab allies fear that the destruction of Iraq would dangerously play into the hands of Iran and Israel and lead to endless regional instability. They also need some movement towards a settlement of the Israeli-Palestinian conflict in order to make their support of American intervention tolerable to their own populations.

Although the United States managed to pressure its Security Council colleagues to go along with its view that the Israeli-Palestinian conflict must be kept apart from the Gulf crisis, there is no likelihood of such a message finding support among the people of the Middle East. Eventually, The United States is going to have to come to terms with the centrality of the Palestinian issue to the region as a whole.

Far more than any other issue, the question of Palestine embodies the resentment that Arab peoples feel toward western domination and their failure to exert control over their own resources and destinies. It is no accident that those countries which have done most to democratize their systems, including America's old friends Jordan and Tunisia, have remained opposed to American intervention. A "solution" which succeeds in getting Iraq out of Kuwait but allows Israel to continue to occupy Palestinian lands in defiance of Security Council resolutions 242 and 338 would only deepen popular resentment of Israel, the United States, and the Arab ruling elites, feed religious fundamentalism or revolutionary nationalism, and keep the region in ferment.

Towards a Just Middle East Policy

Where will the United States stand? How much longer in the post-Cold War world can the United States sustain a foreign policy built around double standards, justifying the magnitude of its support for Israel on the grounds that it is holding the line against Soviet aggression in the Middle East? What role can we play in the creation of a foreign policy which respects the self-determination of peoples, fosters democracy and human rights throughout the region, seeks a consistent implementation of international law and works for an end to the Middle East's viciously spiralling arms race and all its military occupations?

The focus for our activity in helping bring about a just Middle East policy must be Congress—for it is Congress which represents us and Congress which has obstructed past attempts to bring about even minor modifications in the U.S. stance in the region. We must inform ourselves about our representatives' record on fifteen votes and understand the extent of their refusal to take any action which might be construed as against Israel's interest.

We must also recognize the role of Congress in preventing the United States from upholding its own stated policy in the Middle East—a policy which, on paper, includes support for UN resolutions 242 and 338 calling for an Israeli withdrawal from its occupied territories, a determination that Israel as occupier must abide by the Fourth Geneva Convention of 1949, and declared opposition to Israel's annexation of East Jerusalem and settlement program. During the three years of the Palestinian uprising, which have cost the Palestinians the per capita equivalent of some 140,000 American lives and 15 million American wounded, Congress has repeatedly used political intimidation and its control over appropriations to block any meaningful movement towards a resolution of the Israeli-Palestinian conflict. Despite successive State Department reports which could not disguise the pattern of increasingly barbaric human rights abuses committed by Israel and despite the failure of the Israeli government to abide by its own "peace plan," Congress voted substantial increases in U.S. aid to Israel during this period.

The recent record is a sorry one.[10] With few exceptions, our elected representatives have sought successfully to straightjacket and then terminate the U.S.-PLO "dialogue," to prevent any serious examination of Israel's human rights record, to shoot down Senator Dole's "trial balloon" proposing a 5 percent cut across the board to the five largest foreign aid recipients, and to counter the administration's attempts to link U.S. housing loan guarantees to a halt to building settlements in the territories. They have been swift to react to any perceived slight of Israel by the executive branch. And as documented above, they have hastened to tie the administration's hands on the matter of "linkage," apparently preferring the possibility of thousands of American casualties in the Gulf to convening an international peace conference which could mediate region-wide problems.

Making Our Voices Heard

In *They Dare to Speak Out* former Congressperson Paul Findley writes that the Israeli-Palestinian conflict

> is a ticking bomb that grows steadily more dangerous... If our citizens, whether in private life or public office, are able to hear only one side of the issue, they are seriously handicapped as they attempt to define intelligently their interests and set wisely the policies to be followed. From a fettered and unbalanced dialogue truly awful decisions may emerge.[11]

Findley argues that the true interests of both the United States and Israel will be served if citizens "who

favor a more balanced U.S. policy in the Middle East based
on fundamental ideals of justice and peaceful settlement
of international disputes" let their Congresspeople know
that there is more than one side to the story: "The majority
of Congresspeople resent heavy-handed tactics by the
Israeli lobby and will welcome constituent pressure to
modify their habit of voting for whatever Israel wants." [12]

All the traditional forms of influencing our elected
representatives—letters, phone calls, face-to-face meetings—must be employed to let them know that there are
citizens whom it is their paid job to represent who desire
a just and even-handed policy in the Middle East.

But we must at the same time recognize that our
representatives often base their decisions about how to
vote not on the justice of a certain issue, nor on the
expressed views of the people in their district, but according to what best serves the needs of their re-election
campaign. This means that certain citizens, or groups of
citizens, may be more important than others when members make their voting decisions.

Even when Cambridge, Massachusetts voters in
1988 gave majority support to a referendum question
calling for Israel to withdraw from the occupied territories
and for an end to U.S. funds to sustain the occupation,
Joseph Kennedy, who represented the Cambridge constituency, refused to change his stand on Israel. Clearly, the
wishes of his constituents were not the decisive factor in
determining the Congressperson's policy.

Could it be that his policy was shaped more by
money, by campaign contributions? A simple analysis of
Kennedy's campaign contributions through 1988 shows
that he received just over $12,000 from "pro-Israel" Polit-
ical Action Committees (PACs), which gave more than
$3.8 million in direct contributions to the campaigns of
453 candidates in the run-up to the 1988 elections. [13] It is
unlikely that $12,000 was a significant enough sum to

sway a Congressperson.

A deeper analysis would require obtaining a copy of the Congressperson's election statement—available free of charge from the Washington-based Federal Elections Commission. This lists all substantial political contributions from PACs as well as individuals. But only a careful examination of the list by a political insider who can decipher the political motivations of individual donors could tell the whole story. We might discover that a large section of donations were from out of state and feel confident that they were given for "pro-Israel" reasons.

This sort of investigation might help us understand an individual's voting record on Israel, but can it explain the voting patterns which consistently dominate Congress? According to Paul Findley, members of Congress, even those from rural constituencies with only domestic concerns, fear being voted out of office by forces that could be mobilized from around the country if they do not toe the line on Israel. Findley himself and California Democrat Pete McCloskey are two candidates who suffered this fate, as *They Dare to Speak Out* documents.

It is important to understand both the range of pressures being exerted on our elected representatives, and their chief sources of support, and then develop tactics for exerting effective pressure of our own. Our indispensable tool is information. How have our representatives voted on particular Middle East issues?[14] How does a particular Congressional district really work? Which are the most influential institutions within a given constituency?[15] With which organizations and individuals does an elected representative have the strongest ties? Who has given him or her significant campaign contributions? How can we get our message across to individual contributors and to key institutions such as the churches, the media, organized labor and the business community—and use them to build bridges within the political system?

Finally, we must recognize the opportunity we now

have of harnessing the strength of the anti-war movement which we are currently building to the creation of a just policy for the Middle East. As we come together to end armed conflict in the Gulf and bring the troops home, we must simultaneously work to dismantle the region's other "ticking time bomb." For never has it been more clear that peace in the Middle East is "indivisible"—and that piece-meal solutions are no solutions at all.

Notes

1. *MidEast Mirror,* December 13, 1990.

2. Alfred Lilienthal, *The Zionist Connection II* (North American, 1982), p. 253.

3. Alfred Lilienthal, p. 270.

4. Cheryl Rubenberg, Israel and the American National Interest: A Critical Examination (University of Illinois Press, 1986), pp. 3-6.

5. Cheryl Rubenberg, p. 3.

6. *Ma'ariv,* July 7, 1968.

7. See Benjamin Beit-Hallahmi, *The Israeli Connection: Who Israel Arms and Why* (Pantheon Books, 1987) and Jane Hunter, *Israeli Foreign Affairs,* an Independent Monthly Research Report available from PO Box 19580, Sacramento, CA 95819.

8. Paul Findley, They Dare to Speak Out: People and Institutions Confront Israel's Lobby (Lawrence Hill & Company, 1985), p. 101.

9. Paul Findley, p. 102.

10. For detailed information contact The Middle East Justice Network, PO Box 558, Cambridge, MA 02238; tel (617) 666-8061.

11. Paul Findley, p. 320.

12. Paul Findley, p. 328.

13. For a detailed analysis of pro-Israel PACs, see Richard Curtiss, Stealth PACs: How Israel's American Lobby Seeks Control of U.S. Middle East Policy (American Educational Trust, 1990).

14. For a record of how House and Senate members voted on the question of Palestine during 1989-1990 and PAC donations, contact The Middle East Justice Network and ask for its publication *Israel and Palestine: A Congressional Report Card* (1990).

15. For more information about Congressional districts, consult *The Almanac of American Politics,* the National Journal Inc, Washington, DC (202-857-1400). For a detailed analysis of how to shape a lobbying strategy that works through the "pillars of society," contact Peg McCormack at the Arab American Institute (202-429-9210) and request one of her unpublished reports.

Towards a Pro-Democracy Movement in the United States

Randy Kehler

To be effective, we must learn from our past experiences as activists. As a former national coordinator of the Nuclear Weapons Freeze Campaign, Kehler is in a unique position to outline the relevant successes and pitfalls of that effort. He argues that electoral reforms—aimed at the separation of wealth and state—must be made if we are to have a democracy representing the interests of everyone in the United States and capable of implementing some of the structural changes needed to prevent future wars.

As W. H. ("Ping") Ferry has often reminded us, there is no peace movement in this country and there never has been. Yes, says Ferry, we've often had an anti-war movement, or an anti-intervention movement, or a disarmament movement—focused on a particular war, military intervention, or type of weapon—and, Ferry would add, we've often had damn good ones. But we've never had a popular movement that was talking about peace, about something more than stopping war or some aspect of it.

Thanks to the war in the Persian Gulf, this definition of the peace movement is likely to continue at least as long as it takes for a negotiated settlement to be found, the current stalemate to become the new status quo (with temporary U.S. bases in the Gulf having become permanent), an all-out Middle East war to extinguish itself (along with untold thousands of lives), or some combination of these. With so many of us (including this author) feeling compelled to put aside or slow the pace of longer-term work for structural or systemic change while we address the immediate crisis, we find ourselves about to repeat the history of the peace movement once again. What follows is a plea that in the course of fighting the present fire we not abandon our efforts to create fire-resistant structures for the future.

For peace activists to transcend our history, it will require seeing particular wars and war preparations as inherent manifestations of a war system, and then asking ourselves what an equally dynamic, self-sustaining peace system might look like. As soon as we do this, we broaden the traditional definition of peace to include questions of economic justice, ecology and technology, politics and culture. The very complexity that such a definition entails is enough to drive most activists back into single-issue anti-war work. Yet, we must persist in this kind of analysis and prognosis. If we consider that war is not just a matter of battlefields and bullets, but that it has political, economic, cultural, and environmental causes and consequences as well, then we must begin to envision "peace" in similarly complex, integrated terms.

I want to argue that one central element in any robust "peace system" is democracy, or, generally stated, "government of, by, and for the people." Or, put another way, "a politics of human dignity and equality" that affords all citizens equal opportunity to shape the decisions that affect their lives. While there is no such thing as perfect democracy ("One may approach it as one would the horizon...but it can never be attained," said Vaclav Havel in his January 1990 address to Congress), it is partly for lack of a better democracy in the U.S. that the peace movement, and nearly every other progressive movement, has failed to achieve its goals—including the avoidance of war.

The Persian Gulf crisis is itself a case in point. Had we put in place, a decade or two ago, a series of fundamental reforms designed to make the political process serve the public's interests before those of the corporate elite, we might have had energy policies that eliminated our dependence on Middle East oil; we might have begun halting the scandalous international arms trade that has provided countries like Iraq with enormous arsenals of modern weaponry; we might have worked to strengthen, rather than weaken, the United Nations and especially its peace-keeping capabilities (the United States is still three-quarters of a billion dollars in arrears on our UN dues); and the Pentagon might have been forced to scrap its post-Cold War ambitions of "policing 'instability' throughout the Third World" (see Borosage, *The Nation,* September 24, 1990).

The same monied interests that tilted the political playing field away from such policies are very much in the driver's seat today, as the U.S. government responds militarily to Iraq's invasion of Kuwait. The crisis has given the armaments industry, with its thousands of subcontracting businesses, a new lease on life. What is their influence within policy-making circles? The oil industry stands to reap windfall profits if prices continue to rise and the demand for more domestic oil forces a lifting of environmental restrictions on offshore drilling. How loud is *their* voice in the ears of congressional and White House decision-makers?

The sad fact, with few if any exceptions, is that even when we have citizen's movements supported by overwhelming popular majorities, they can rarely muster as much political clout in Washington (or state capitals) as do the wealthy vested interests who finance the re-election campaigns of our selected representatives. The Freeze campaign was a great example of this anti-democratic phenomenon, but it's the same story whether we're talking about nuclear disarmament or universal health care, jobs for minority youth or intervention in Central America, ozone depletion or low-income housing, capital gains taxes or Middle East policy.

This is not a new problem; George Washington as well as Lyndon Johnson is said to have "bought" his first election to public office. But it is now a worse problem, if only because the skyrocketing costs of today's television-oriented electoral races (Jim Hightower said he would have had to raise at least $15 million to run against Texas Senator Phil Gramm in November 1990) make politicians more dependent than ever on those who give or round up large sums of money. As Wisconsin labor organizer and ex-U.S. Senate candidate Ed Garvey puts it, "Private money in election campaigns is eating at the guts of our entire political process." The S&L debacle is but one tragic result of such a process.

The problem of "money in politics" is so deeply ingrained, and our public officials so caught up in it (albeit with decreasing enthusiasm), that Congress and state legislatures will never adopt serious democratic reform until they feel the heat of sustained grassroots pressure from a broad-based (and absolutely nonpartisan) citizen's movement—a U.S. pro-democracy movement. In order to inspire such a movement, however, proposals for reform must be bold and comprehensive. None of the current reforms being debated in Washington meet this test. Not one puts caps on campaign spending. Not cheaper television rates for campaign commercials. Not even the abolition of all Political Action Committees (PACs), which would simply drive up contributions from wealthy individuals representing the same interests. And not even partial public financing, which subsidizes rather than eliminates the "money chase."

While a U.S. pro-democracy movement must expose a range of basic demands, including non-electoral ones, there can be none more important than the virtual elimination of all private money in public elections. If private

money—because it is so unequally and unjustly distrib-
uted—is not a suitable medium for political democracy,
then no private money whatsoever should be allowed.
Instead, public elections should be financed entirely with
public money.

The cost of such a scheme—$5-10 per year per tax-
payer to provide total public financing for all congressional and presidential candidates—would be but a
fraction of what the current system is costing us. If media
reform were added to the reform package—e.g., mandat-
ing that the highly profitable television industry provide
eligible candidates with free and equal access to the public
airwaves—the cost might be cut in half. If we compare this
with the several thousand dollars per taxpayer that the
S&L bailout alone will cost us (not to mention the many
other multi-billion-dollar legislative heists caused at least
in part by politicians' dependence on their campaign contributors), total public financing is a bargain-basement
deal.

Eliminating privately-financed election campaigns
would constitute a "sea change" in the way politics in the
United States has traditionally been conducted. It would
mean that anyone capable of attracting public support—
i.e., by gathering a required number of petition signatures
or endorsement cards—could run a competitive campaign
for major public office, regardless of whether that person
had lots of money or the ability to raise it. It would mean
that candidates, instead of spending most of their time
and energy raising money, could spend it, in Hightower's
words, on "raising issues, raising hopes, and raising hell."
And, most important, it would mean that elected officials,
once in office, would be much freer to make public policy
on the basis of public interests rather than those of their
private financial backers. It is hard to imagine a reform
that would have more far-reaching ramifications.

The Supreme Court, in its 1976 *Buckley v. Valeo*
decision, erroneously equated campaign expenditures

with free speech, and ruled that any limitation on such expenditures is unconstitutional except as a condition placed on the voluntary acceptance of public money. For this reason, the system of total public financing advocated here would have to be voluntary. Candidates who opt for public financing could not accept any private contributions and thus their expenditures would be limited to the amount of public financing received. It is unlikely that any candidate would turn down such an option, even if philosophically opposed to it. In the eighteen years since the institution of partial public financing for presidential elections (a piecemeal reform that in no way ended candidates' and parties' dependence on big money contributors) only one unsuccessful primary candidate has turned the money down.

The creation of the U.S. pro-democracy movement capable of bringing about such reform will depend on at least three factors. One is already in place: dramatic "pro-democracy" movements in Eastern Europe, the Soviet Union, South Africa, China, Burma, Chile, and elsewhere, that have created a propitious global climate in which Americans have already begun to re-examine the quality and equality of democracy in the U.S. A second factor has to do with our own domestic situation. As conditions which directly affect people's lives continue to worsen—for example, the unemployment-drugs-and-violence syndrome in our inner cities, the toxic poisoning of rural communities, deteriorating public schools and diminishing social services nearly everywhere—more and more people are noticing the corruption and bankruptcy of our political system and its transparent inability to solve or even address these problems.

While these two factors are out of our control, the third is not. This one has to do with deliberate steps we can take to organize and map out a program for a U.S. pro-democracy movement which can flourish in the evolving national and global environment described above. For better or worse, there is no definitive science of social movements; like the individuals and groups that compose them, social movements must be seen as constantly evolving, organic entities whose life cycles are predictable only in the most general sense at best. Nevertheless, there are lessons to be learned from past movements and, with some humility, applied to future ones.

In thinking about the creation of a pro-democracy movement, a number of lessons come to my mind from the recent experience of the nuclear disarmament movement and, in particular, the Freeze Campaign.

- Paint the big picture at the outset, especially if most of the emphasis is initially placed on one specific reform. Make clear where that reform—be it a halt in nuclear weapons production or the abolition of privately financed election campaigns—is expected to lead, and what other, related reforms are necessary. Otherwise, the target reform becomes an end in itself and is more vulnerable to derailment or cooptation.

- Err on the side of too much rather than too little time spent building the movement's grassroots base of support. Particularly in light of the anti-democratic political clout of corporate money in the policy-making arenas, social movements cannot hope to succeed without enormous grassroots strength. This translates into good old-fashioned community organizing and the creation of sturdy community organizations and organizational coalitions.

- Don't believe your own press. One of the reasons why the Freeze Campaign turned to the congressional arena too soon was because we believed what *Time* and *Newsweek* were saying about us—that this was the largest, most powerful movement in recent U.S. history. A prairie fire of citizen protest that was taking Washington by storm. Nonsense. A sensational story that sold lots of magazines. The strength of our public support was a mile wide but still only an inch deep, and politicians knew it.

- Don't make grassroots lobbying of Congress (or state legislatures) the primary task movement supporters are called upon to perform—even when it is time to focus on legislation. As the Freeze Campaign discovered, lobbying alone does not sustain, much less build, a social movement. Instead, it tends to remove the issue from the communities where people live and work and reinforces the notion that change can only happen if "they"—the elites in Washington or the state capital—make it happen. Instead, a healthy movement requires actions that can be taken locally, and that can bring about some degree of change locally. In effect, we make the change, and our elected representatives, faced with no other alternative, simply turn it into legislation. Devising meaningful local actions with which to build a pro-democracy movement will be a challenge.

- Create clear litmus tests, and define our own victories. Early on, the Freeze Campaign tried to make clear that reductions in nuclear weapons, in the absence of a halt to continued production, was unacceptable. But in later years, in the wake of ballyhooed summit meetings and "dramatic" proposals for 50-100 percent reductions, the Campaign joined in the acclaim, albeit critically, and thus lost its cutting edge. (And to date, despite some minor reductions of already-deployed weapons, not a sin-

gle new nuclear weapon system has been halted.)
Similarly, today's proposals for band-aid reforms of
the campaign finance system constitute a distrac-
tion at best and a step backward at worst. Sometimes what looks like half a loaf is no loaf at all.

- Most important of all, create a diverse, multi-racial
  movement from the outset. Movements that are
  primarily white and white-collar, as the Freeze was
  (and the environmental movement is), find it nearly
  impossible to attract blue-collar workers and people
  of color to their ranks—even when we try (and,
  more often than not, we don't). Any relatively homogeneous group will naturally adopt its own cul-
  turally-defined language and mode of operation,
  and it should come as no surprise that people of
  other cultural norms feel excluded.

The rationale for creating a diverse movement is not
simply, or even primarily, a matter of mustering additional political strength, as important as that is. An even
more compelling reason is that racism and other forms of
prejudice are probably the most insidious and destructive
of all the ills our society faces—and they are on the rise.
For that reason, it is doubly important that a nascent
pro-democracy movement—which, like all other social
movements, must be seen essentially as a liberation movement—break out of society's cultural divisions right from
the beginning. Diversity, particularly racial diversity,
must characterize the leadership as well as the member-
ship of this new movement, both locally and nationally.

This will, no doubt, be the most difficult challenge of
all, but one well worth taking on. What should make it
easier is the fact that fundamental reform of our system
of political democracy is in nearly everyone's interest. It
has the potential to join all of the issues all of us care about
and thereby cut across all of the boundaries that separate

us.

If we want to see crises elsewhere in the world defused peaceably rather than used as excuses for military buildups, then we must democratize the political process. If we want decent, affordable housing available to all, then we must insist on equal political opportunity for people without wealth or the ability to raise it. If we want to see health care become a universal right, then we must create a political system in which well-financed medical and pharmaceutical lobbies do not have disproportionate influence. If we want every young person looking for work to have a meaningful job at a reasonable wage, then we must give equal political voice to the unemployed. If we want to prevent future S&L disasters and make the wealthy pay their fair share of this one, then we must demand a separation of wealth and state. If we want to protect and restore the quality of our air, water, and soil before current deterioration becomes irreversible, then we must make sure that the election campaigns of our public servants are not financed by corporate polluters. And, if we have any hope of our country ever standing in solidarity with people who are poor and oppressed in other countries, then we certainly must make good on the principle of "government of, by, and for the people" here at home.

Beyond Crisis Response

Building a Peace System

Robert A. Irwin

What are the tasks facing those who wish to do more than restrain the excesses of U.S. foreign policy and who seek to change the social and political power structures that give rise to crises such as that in the Persian Gulf? Irwin puts forth a powerful argument that we should create a vision of a world that can exist peacefully, study the forces working for and against that future, and develop and implement strategies to achieve our goal. As he suggests, working backwards from an imagined point in the future can help us recognize neglected yet doable tasks that we should undertake now to bring that future into being.

He observes that "This chapter has been written without knowing the outcome of the Gulf War begun on January 16, 1991. While that ignorance is a disadvantage for an author wanting to tailor his presentation to the likely state of mind of readers, it symbolizes one of the themes of this chapter: that despite uncertainties about the future course of events, intelligent strategizing can be done."

Responding rapidly and effectively to crises like the war in the Persian Gulf is important. But without changing the political, economic, and social structures that allow and encourage these crises to occur, we are at best only delaying disaster.

Conflicts in human society are as inevitable as earthquakes—and far more frequent. We cannot wish them away. But we need a system for dealing with them that is less destructive than war. Envisioning such a system may seem difficult in a world constantly torn by war. Yet it is a crucial project.[1]

"But, wait," someone may object. "Urgent life-and-death struggles require our energies. We must deal with the real world, not with what we wish were the case. We cannot afford to waste time fantasizing about a utopian world of peace."

Restraining U.S. involvement in Vietnam, Central America, and elsewhere has been important, and we must continue to respond to crises. But why make time to do visionary thinking? There are three important reasons.

First, envisioning and articulating alternatives to present policies helps persuade people and involve them in the struggle for change. The kind of disciplined visionary thinking advocated here means a careful elaboration of the alternatives we propose to the status quo. How practically relevant—how crucial—it is to put forth alternatives is easily shown: polls cited December 12, 1990 indicated that the U.S. public only supported use of military force against Iraq when no alternative (such as giving sanctions time to work) was mentioned by the pollster.[2]

Second (as countless volumes on planning, management, and self-help rightly insist), clarity about our goals is essential to enable us to work toward them effectively. To the degree that our goal is unclear, we do not know what we are working for when we work for peace, and may make needless mistakes from short-sightedness. For example, the focus on nuclear weapons disarmament must be broadened if we are to build a movement capable of preventing war.

Finally, the more vivid our goal, the more it will inspire us, motivate us, and sustain our morale over the time required to accomplish it. This is true even though the goal we achieve will doubtless differ from our original vision.[3]

There is, then, nothing escapist or trivial about im-

proving our ability to win public support through offering
alternatives, clarifying our goals, enabling us to make
better decisions on strategy, and sustaining our motivation by keeping our "eyes on the prize."

Admittedly, in a crisis alternatives need to be
summed up briefly: "Sanctions, not war!" gets the gist
across. But permanently eliminating war and other violence from human society requires a more elaborate vision
and a comprehensive strategy translated into doable
tasks.

Aspects of a Peace System

What are the elements of a vision capable of dealing
with inevitable social and international conflicts? The
term adopted here—"peace system"—signifies that peacemaking is a dynamic, complex process of dealing with
conflicts and problems in ways that prevent war and
minimize suffering. A comprehensive peace system would
involve institutions, policies, and practices growing out of
initiatives at many levels from local to global. The term
does not imply something totally formalized or imposed
by an authority.[4]

Since peace and war do not result only from political
and legal structures, and since war is not the only evil that
damages human well-being, a peace system must take
into account ecological, economic, and cultural factors as
well. To transform the present war system—a system that
regularly produces war and other suffering—into a peace
system requires changes in all these inter-related realms.

To begin with the political and legal: part of a peace
system must be processes of collective self-governance at
the global level. The United Nations could be a reasonable
approximation of a global governance institution, but it is
severely hampered by the Security Council veto power
held by the U.S., U.S.S.R., U.K., France, and China.
Reforming its voting system (which should become part of

the agenda of progressive activists) would enable the U.N. to go much further in living up to its potential.[5]

In a world often subjected to the rule of force, one might assume international law to be too limited to be of use. On the contrary, the period since 1945 has been a time of great progress in global codification of legal and human rights principles. While more legislation on the international level could be helpful, it is important to realize that many of the violent acts that activists work to stop are already defined as illegal by international law. The U.S. invasions of Grenada and Panama, the Israeli occupation of the West Bank and Gaza, and the U.S. funding of the contras were all illegal by current standards. The U.N., along with the World Court, international law, and various specialized U.N. agencies and institutions, serves as the center of a rudimentary global governance system.

Despite a solid legal structure and significant use of U.N. peacekeeping forces (awarded the 1988 Nobel Peace Prize), enforcement of global law has been thwarted time and again, often by the United States, which has in the past 20 years vetoed more Security Council resolutions than any other member.[6] In a well-functioning peace system, international law usually would be abided by, and in case of violations, effectively enforced. We will return to the issue of enforcement as it relates to activists below.

Preventing war will depend not only on political and legal changes, but on altering the economic and ecological status quo as well. The presently dominant economic system, capitalism, is not sustainable: it is destroying its own basis.[7] An economic system, to be consistent with durable peace, should be secure, sustainable, and satisfying. Making subsistence completely secure should be top priority, and reduction of global economic inequality would be a high priority in the building of a peace system. As has been pointed out by the Institute for Food and Development Policy, food production and distribution could be reorganized to provide healthy food for everyone. A primary goal should be to insulate subsistence from economic fluctuations and market forces that affect degrees of prosperity and luxury. Without a basic floor of subsistence, war cannot be eliminated as a means for resolving conflict.[8]

The traditional views of what constitutes foreign aid and development must be challenged, as Frances Moore Lappé has done when she argues that "aid" is often in reality an obstacle to meeting the needs of those it is supposed to help.[9] Fortunately, solid success stories of internally-generated participatory development provide an alternative.[10] It is the responsibility of those concerned with peace to examine the nature of aid programs of the industrialized nations and demand programs that support participatory development.

Sustainability is, by definition, necessary for secure subsistence to last. Often, economic health is viewed as opposed to ecological concerns. It is argued that we simply cannot afford to protect the environment because it will cost too many jobs, and controlling pollution is too expensive. Such arguments do not adequately reckon ecological costs. As the Worldwatch Institute has pointed out, the ability of an economic order to meet the needs of its people is intimately tied to and dependent on sustainable use of resources.

Finally, an economic system must be capable of satisfying the wants to which it gives rise, or else it will be rejected. As Andre Gorz, Murray Bookchin, and others have pointed out, the meaningless drudgery which constitutes work life for many could be reduced or eliminated. The system most conducive to peace—one that would produce desired goods efficiently, enhance political democracy, promote tolerance in individuals, and encourage people to work fewer hours and be less acquisitive—would involve workplace democracy and an institutional setting of less concentrated ownership that is more complex than can be summarized here.[11]

The culture underlying a peace system must incorporate a feminist ethic of caring and concern for life as an essential element. Peace and feminism are profoundly linked. As Elise Boulding has written, "the template of patriarchy as a social institution continues to mold generation after generation,...continuing the practice of warfare and the subjection of women." [12] We must replace a culture that exalts competition with one that fosters cooperation. Such a society, psychology suggests, would be "more congruent with human nature than the one we now have." [13] In a humane, multicultural world, people would strive to afford one another respect based on mutual understanding even where strong disagreements existed.

One crucial aspect of culture is how information flows. As Noam Chomsky, Edward Herman, and others have shown, the media corporations determine what news is widely available, and confine debate to a narrow spectrum which rarely permits fundamental challenges to the current political, social, and economic order. Supporting alternative channels of information and education is a key task in creating a peace system.[14]

The changes required to build a peace system—envisioning how a peaceful world could exist, reforming the U.N. to be a more effective guardian of human rights and international law, eliminating gross economic inequalities, implementing an ecologically sustainable economy, and having a multicultural and informed society—are massive. To many, a peace system may seem nothing more than a hopeless wish. How can a coherent strategy be built that seeks to achieve these changes?

Strategic Thinking

Thinking strategically isn't easy to do, but why it is difficult is easy to understand. Good strategic thinking requires having a clear goal in mind, understanding the forces working for and against achievement of that goal (and how one might influence them), anticipating the likely reactions to actions taken toward the goal, and estimating how to use one's situation and resources to best advantage. That means being something of a visionary, social scientist, chess player, and manager all at once.

In local and short-term campaigns for change, many aspects of the situation may be taken as fixed—as givens. But for any large goals, requiring time, the national and global situations, with all their complexity and unpredictability, are themselves variables—unknowns—that will influence the forces one is strategizing about.

The limits on how much knowledge one can acquire, and on how well one can forecast what the world's complexities are going to mean for one's efforts, are unavoidable constraints to strategizing. Nevertheless, books like this one (and magazines, and political education in general) can help by providing information about the global and national situations, and by offering ideas, frameworks, and intellectual tools that suggest what's most important to pay attention to and how to analyze it.[15]

Some of the most useful of these can only be mentioned here, but are valuable for both experienced and beginning activists: Bill Moyer's "Movement Action Plan," outlining the typical stages of social movements, and his "Four Roles of Activism" model; and George Lakey's five-stage model for how fundamental social change can be brought about.[16]

Strategy and Nonviolent Struggle

Every strategy for political change rests on assumptions about the nature of political power. If power grows out of the barrel of a gun, as Mao asserted, strategy for change would seem ultimately to depend on successful warfare. If power grows out of elections, strategy should be oriented to winning them.[17]

However, the most insightful theory finds power to depend ultimately on obedience: willingness to pull the gun's trigger, willingness to obey the elected official or policeman. When that obedience is withheld on a mass scale, political power sometimes crumbles, or changes hands. Eastern Europe in 1989 and the Philippines in 1986 provided widely noted examples.

Deliberate use of nonviolent struggle puts this theory of power into practice. But "nonviolence" is much misunderstood. There are more than half a dozen distinguishable types of rejection of violence on principle, and they vary greatly in origins, goals, and degree of militancy.[18] Nonviolent struggle as a technique encompasses some 200 methods, ranging from the silent vigil and the solitary fast to sit-ins, boycotts, strikes, mass demonstrations, and wholesale refusal of citizens, officials, and military forces to do what they're told.[19]

The frequency and sophistication of nonviolent struggle seem gradually to be increasing, and in a century where science has multiplied the social and ecological destructiveness of warfare, the case for a strategic commitment to nonviolent struggle deserves careful study by all who seek fundamental change.[20]

Building a Peace System: A Strategic Framework

Striving for world peace conceived as a state of conflict-free harmony is unrealistic. We should instead seek to build a peace system: a global condition in which many of today's kinds of conflicts (rooted in desperate privation or ruthless exploitation) are totally absent, many emerging conflicts are resolved peaceably through negotiated agreement, and unresolved acute conflicts are waged by nonviolent struggle.

It is essential that people opposed to U.S. military

interventionism and nuclear arsenals devote energy to exploring the nature of the institutions, policies, practices, economics, and culture of a world handling its conflicts without war and oppression. The idea that we are trying to *build* something, not merely to *resist* and raise the costs of crimes committed by the U.S. government, has important implications for what we do (and even for guiding our resistance).

Many of the elements of a better future exist embryonically in the present. Compared to the scale of global problems, they may seem insignificant. Yet they languish (or grow too slowly) because we do not recognize the importance of nurturing them. Certain U.N. agencies, humanitarian organizations such as Peace Brigades International, and many economic institutions with a logic superior to communism and capitalism are examples.[21]

Each major element of a future peace system requires careful strategizing in its own right; generalizations risk being superficial and unconvincing. But for each element there are things activists can do—sometimes easy things—that move us a little closer to peace.[22]

Enforcing International Law: A Strategy Example

Here is one example of peace system strategizing. A reasonable vision of global peace includes the idea of military invasions being illegal. (The U.N. Charter, in fact, already prohibits such behavior.) As noted above, enforcement is largely ineffective today; invasions are not uncommon, and rarely undone or punished. While a full solution to this problem will require major changes in global politics (of such magnitude as perhaps to discourage us from even thinking about it), starting with a mental journey into the future and envisioning the goal as already achieved can suggest to us ideas usable now by activists and not dependent on the occurrence of dreamed-of changes.

In a well-functioning peace system, one of many reasons war would not occur would be that citizens in every country would feel personally responsible for seeing that their government did not violate international law. If we think backward toward the present, seeking the seeds that would have grown into such a universal citizen attitude, we may consider that possibly *even now* we have such a responsibility for our government's behavior.

Investigation in fact reveals that, in the opinion of at least a few distinguished legal scholars, present laws already prohibit as illegal such U.S. policies as deployment of nuclear weapons and support for one side in El Salvador's civil war.[23]

These thoughts lead us to notice other seeds. We discover that those people who have felt obliged to undertake nonviolent direct action on grounds of conscience against nuclear weapons or U.S. Central America policy have increasingly also invoked the Nuremberg Principles (adopted by the U.S. and other World War II victors as the legal basis for prosecuting Nazi crimes) as part of the justification for their actions.

There is already more evidence than most activists realize that juries will accept these arguments and grant acquittals to defendants nonviolently blocking arms shipments or disrupting operation of government offices.[24] If growing numbers of activists cite international law as the basis for opposing criminal U.S. government policies (as has been happening), we will thereby both increase U.S. public awareness of the global legal order and of criminal acts by our government and transmit the message that all citizens have an obligation to secure compliance with the law.

Thus we will advance toward our long-term vision while resisting the specific violations of that vision in the present. Like participants in the student sit-in movement of the early 1960s, we will be demonstrating in the present the values and behaviors of the future we desire.[25]

Next Steps That Can Be Taken Immediately

Although a comprehensive strategic framework like "building a peace system" has numerous implications, just four next steps are offered here so that each reader will end the chapter with a sense of specific things to do next. These steps will be useful regardless of what happens in the Persian Gulf.

1. Make continuous self-education a priority. This chapter's notes are full of suggestions for further learning. Before setting this book down, choose one (or more) to act on this week. Improving your routine information sources through appropriate subscriptions and organizational ties is highly important.[26] Talk to other people about what you learn, and learn from that dialogue as well.

2. Exercise your imagination with visionary thinking. Contact someone who runs workshops on imaging the future.[27] Learn to think strategically. Consider forming a group to study peace and related issues.[28]

3. Participate in "nonviolence training." You may not feel ready to participate in nonviolent direct action; maybe you've never even taken part in a demonstration before. But if you want to see the world move toward peace, you should get acquainted firsthand with the nature of the "people power" that's making history around the world. You may be able to locate a nonviolence trainer with half a dozen phone calls or less. (Be persistent.) Try your local peace group (if you know of one) or call a national one to get names of trainers in your part of the U.S.[29]

4. Join and become active with one or two groups, preferably a national one and a local one.[30] National groups can keep you informed and help you feel connected to many others. If you don't know of any local group, try starting one. Post a flier in public places, giving a phone number and announcing a meeting. If no one responds, try it again later. For more detailed advice on organizing, excellent handbooks are available.[31]

Self-education, developing action skills, linking up with others—these are emphasized here because they will be useful no matter what specifics the future holds. Such actions in the present will be useful for responding to crises, yet equally consistent with recognition of the long-term change needed for going beyond crisis response and building a peace system.

Notes

1. The ideas mentioned in this chapter, plus additional ones and many leads for further study and action, are developed in more detail in Robert A. Irwin, *Building a Peace System* (ExPro Press, 1989). That book grew out of the work of the Exploratory Project on the Conditions of Peace (ExPro), founded in 1984 to encourage more of the long-range goal and strategy thinking for which busy activists have difficulty finding time. The book is specially designed for use by study groups as well as individuals. It can be ordered through a bookstore or, in bulk, from The Talman Company, 150 Fifth Ave., New York, NY 10011; (212) 620-3182.

2. Cited on "All Things Considered," National Public Radio, December 18, 1990.

3. For more on visioning, see *Building a Peace System* (hereafter cited as *BAPS*), pp. 35-45; for information on resource persons who can assist in conducting the "imaging" workshops on envisioning a world without war pioneered by Elise Boulding and Warren Ziegler, see pp. 257-258.

4. See "The Peace System Approach to Eliminating War" in *BAPS*, pp. 1-8.

5. For an assessment of the implications of possible U.N. voting reforms, see Hanna Newcombe, *Design for a Better World* (University Press of America, 1983), pp. 33-101, 127-131, and *BAPS*, p. 52.

6. Noam Chomsky, "The New World Order," public lecture, M.I.T., December 1990. The number of U.S. vetoes in the past twenty years, Chomsky stated, exceeds those of the U.S.S.R., U.K., France, and China by a wide margin, but this fact is not published in the U.S. press. For some particulars, see Chomsky, *Necessary Illusions: Thought Control in Democratic Societies* (South End, 1989), p. 218. See also Norman Finkelstein, "Double Standards in the Gulf," *Z Magazine* (November 1990), pp. 27-28.

7. See the annual *State of the World* volumes by Lester R. Brown et al. for an overview of major ecological problems.

8. For more on the points in this paragraph, see "Economic Development, Ecology, and Peace," in *BAPS*, pp. 63-76, 178-187.

9. See Frances Moore Lappé et al., *Aid as Obstacle* (San Fran-

cisco: Institute for Food and Development Policy, 1981) and Lappé and Joseph Collins, *Food First: Beyond the Myth of Scarcity* (Ballantine, rev. ed., 1978).

10. The world's two most important examples of participatory development are Spain's Mondragon complex and Bangladesh's Grameen Bank. At Mondragon, one five-person cooperative founded in 1955 has become a cluster of over 100 worker cooperatives and supporting organizations (a bank, a technical school) employing nearly 20,000 persons, while retaining democratic management. William F. and Kathleen King Whyte, *Making Mondragon* (ILR Press, 1988) is the best recent account. The Grameen [Village] Bank loans money to the very poor while assisting them in creating self-help structures that support them to start small businesses and improve their housing, diet, sanitation, and general well-being. In its first ten years (1976-86), the Bank helped some one million people lift themselves above abject poverty. Its approach is now being applied in other countries, including the United States. See Andreas Fuglesang and Dale Chandler, *Participation as Process: What We Can Learn from Grameen Bank, Bangladesh* (1986; 234 pp.; free on request from Norwegian Ministry for Development Cooperation, NORAD, Information Unit, P.O. Box 8142-Dep, 0033 Oslo 1, Norway). Both owe their success to idealistic leadership and structures carefully designed to serve both the individual and the common good; both creatively combine the best of capitalist and socialist ideals. See *BAPS*, pp. 73, 185-6, 287-88 for additional details.

11. See *BAPS* pp. 73, 83-84, 181-186 for more specifics. Leland Stauber's *A New Program for Democratic Socialism: Lessons from the Market-Planning Experience in Austria* (Carbondale, IL: Four Willows Press, 1987; 412 pp.) is an original and unduly neglected proposal for reducing concentration of ownership (summarized in *BAPS*, p. 180, note 11).

12. Elise Boulding, "Two Cultures of Religion as Obstacles to Peace," *Zygon* (December 1986), quoted in *BAPS*, p. 81.

13. Robert R. Holt, "Converting the War System to a Peace System: Some Contributions from Psychology and Other Social Sciences" (1987), quoted in *BAPS*, p. 83. For a lucid discussion of relevant scientific research, see Alfie Kohn's *No Contest: The*

Case Against Competition (Houghton Mifflin, 1986) and *The Brighter Side of Human Nature: Altruism and Empathy in Everyday Life* (Basic Books, 1990).

14. For analysis of media bias, see Edward S. Herman and Noam Chomsky, *Manufacturing Consent: The Political Economy of the Mass Media* (Pantheon, 1988); Chomsky, *Necessary Illusions: Thought Control in Democratic Societies* (South End, 1989); interview with Noam Chomsky in *The Humanist* (November-December 1990). Fairness and Accuracy in Reporting (FAIR) exposes the right-wing and centrist slant of the corporate media and describes encouraging successes in combating bias in its newsletter *Extra!* (request sample issue from FAIR, 130 West 25th St., New York, NY 10001).

15. The best single source for an overview of global and domestic U.S. issues is *Future Survey Annual,* which each year summarizes some 700 books and articles. Priced at $25, this extraordinary resource is a bargain for an individual and something every public library should be urged to acquire. To obtain it (or the monthly *Future Survey)*, contact World Future Society Book Service, 4916 St. Elmo Avenue, Bethesda, MD 20814 (301-656-8274).

16. Bill Moyer's "Movement Action Plan (MAP)" indicates the distinct pitfalls and opportunities associated with each stage of a social movement and suggests what activists should be watching for as they appraise their movement's options at each juncture. (Sixteen tabloid-size pages; available for $2.00 postpaid from Social Movement Empowerment Project, 721 Shrader St., San Francisco, CA 94117; 415-387-3361.)

George Lakey's *Powerful Peacemaking: A Strategy for a Living Revolution* (1973; rev. ed., New Society, 1987) is indispensable reading for all who believe that fundamental change will be needed in the United States and in other countries in order to make a peaceful world. Lakey discusses cultural preparation, building organizational strength, (nonviolent) "propaganda of the deed," mass political and economic noncooperation, and finally, intervention to create parallel institutions which contest with the government for the public's allegiance. Lakey's book, written for a U.S. audience, provides the best framework for understanding events like the Eastern Europe regime changes in 1989, yet is global in perspective and rich in insights useful in any society.

One simple but valuable strategizing tool is "Force Field Analysis," explained in Virginia Coover, et al., *Resource Manual for a Living Revolution* (New Society, 1981), pp. 256-257. See also André Gorz's concept of "revolutionary reform," explained on pp. 29-31.

17. That elections in the United States are dominated by a power elite which "operates within—not outside—the democratic process, including the two-party system" is convincingly argued by G. William Domhoff in his *Who Rules America Now?* (Prentice-Hall, 1983; quote from p. 119). See also "The Candidate Selection Process" in Domhoff, *The Powers That Be: Processes of Ruling Class Domination in America* (Vintage, 1979).

"In terms of electoral participation the United States was far more democratic—both on its own terms, and in comparison to Europe—in the 19th century than it is today," Joshua Cohen and Joel Rogers assert in *Rules of the Game: American Politics and the Central America Movement* (South End, 1986), p. 24.

The change is attributed by Frances Fox Piven and Richard A. Cloward to Southern planters and Northern businessmen who introduced poll taxes, literacy requirements, and in-person registration (and, in the South, violent intimidation) to reduce voting; see their *Why Americans Don't Vote* (Pantheon, 1988). Contrary to explanations stressing "apathy," Piven and Cloward show that 88 percent of *registered* U.S. voters voted in 1984, a turnout comparable to European levels, where many more are registered. They conclude that one prerequisite for revitalizing U.S. democracy is European-style universal registration (preface to 1989 paperback edition).

18. See Gene Sharp, "Types of Principled Nonviolence," pp. 201-234 in *Gandhi as a Political Strategist* (Porter Sargent, 1979), for six types, without even distinguishing (for example) Christian and Buddhist nonviolence. Today one should definitely add to Sharp's list feminist (or ecofeminist) nonviolence; see Pam McAllister, ed., *Reweaving the Web of Life: Feminism and Nonviolence* (New Society, 1982).

19. On nonviolent struggle as a technique, the best source is Gene Sharp's three-volume *The Politics of Nonviolent Action* (Porter Sargent, 1973). The theory that power depends on obedience is outlined on pp. 7-32. Volumes Two and Three treat the

methods and dynamics of nonviolent action, with a wealth of historical examples. For other books on nonviolent struggle, contact the War Resisters League and New Society Publishers (see note 31).

20. The pragmatic case for a strategic commitment to nonviolent struggle is best made by Lakey (*Powerful Peacemaking*) and Sharp (see *Social Power and Political Freedom*, Porter Sargent, 1980, pp. 285-378, among his other works). The works of Martin Luther King, Jr. and M. K. Gandhi add religious arguments to the pragmatic ones. Other important authors include Dave Dellinger (*Revolutionary Nonviolence; More Power Than We Know*) and Barbara Deming (*Revolution and Equilibrium; We Are All Part of One Another; Prisons That Could Not Hold*). See *BAPS* pp. 165-166 (notes 25-27) and p. 201 (notes 16-17) for other references.

The case for nonviolent struggle in contrast to political violence in North American societies has recently gained new support. Bob Altemeyer's *Enemies of Freedom: Understanding Right-Wing Authoritarianism* (Jossey-Bass, 1988) is an award-winning, ground-breaking investigation in which the author, through years of psychological testing of students, their parents, and even politicians, has refined a measure of authoritarianism, illuminated its essential elements and its origins, and reached important (and surprising) conclusions on how it can be reduced. Serious activists should become familiar with this study. Most pertinent here:

> The cards are stacked in favor of right-wing extremists if social order dissolves and organized violence and terrorism erupt in the street—especially if the demagogues on the right can blame their excesses on the radical left, which would happen quite naturally. Thus leftists who resort to such tactics would seem to be playing into their enemies' hands. I would call this the "Nixon trap."
> But nonviolent protest may be the trump card of left-wing reformers.... When governments try to suppress peaceful protest movements with force, they appear to trigger a backlash against themselves. This might be called the "Gandhi trap" [p. 310].

"Commitment to nonviolent struggle" was contrasted with violence above. But it is equally important to make the case for the legitimacy and desirability of nonviolent struggle that includes illegal actions (or apparently "illegal"—see Boyle below), as contrasted with confinement to the "moderate," exclusively legal electoral politics dominated by the rich and other entrenched authorities. Societies we now view as models of moderation needed turbulent, disruptive nonviolent struggle to become what they are. George Lakey writes: "A century ago Sweden had poverty, slums, low wages for workers, and little democracy. Now [1973; alas, how much truer in 1991!—RAI] Sweden...looks in comparison to the United States like a kind of paradise." For reasons that Lakey outlines, it was easier to change Sweden than the United States. "But the interesting thing about Sweden as an easier case is that, *even there,* massive direct action was required to force substantial change. A general strike in 1902, then again in 1909, and again in 1931, with accompanying demonstrations, finally dislodged the Swedish power elite enough to put Sweden on its present path toward justice and equality." *Strategy for a Living Revolution* (1973), p. 27 (this passage omitted from the 1987 edition entitled *Powerful Peacemaking*).

It was through nonviolent struggle—not elections—that women and African-Americans won their present voting rights in the U.S. See Robert Irwin, "Nonviolent Struggle and Democracy in American History," *Freeze Focus* (September 1984). Nonviolent struggle will likely be needed again to mobilize sufficient power to bring meaningful election reform in the U.S.

A neglected strategic conception (somewhat akin to Gorz's "revolutionary reforms") is "revolution in stages," as advocated by Sidney Lens in *The Promise and Pitfalls of Revolution* (Pilgrim Press, 1974), pp. 239-264. Denmark's "revolution, proceeding in stages over the course of many decades" (see pp. 34-35), deserves more study in the U.S. See Marquis W. Childs, *Sweden: The Middle Way* (1936 and later editions), for a readable discussion of both Sweden and Denmark.

21. For information on Peace Brigades International, contact PBI, c/o Traprock Peace Center, Keets Road, Deerfield, MA 01342. Another group whose work aids many to move toward a peace system economy is Co-op America, 2100 M St., NW,

Washington, DC 20063; 800-424-COOP or 202-872-5307.

22. For several steps most individuals can take, see *BAPS*, pp. 181-184. To mention just one here: if you use a credit card, you can switch to a Working Assets Visa card that generates money for social change work each time you use it; call 1-800-533-FUND.

23. See Francis Anthony Boyle, *Defending Civil Resistance Under International Law* (1987; 379 pp.; available for $9.00 postpaid from Center for Energy Research, 333 State St., Salem, OR 97301; 503-371-8002; or from *The Nuclear Resister*, P.O. Box 43383, Tucson, AZ 85733). Law professor Richard Falk's introduction states that:

> To disobey is no longer, as with Thoreau, to engage in "civil disobedience," an initiative designed to point up the discrepancy between "law" and "morality," and the priority of the latter for a person of conscience. Such a tension no longer exists. To resist reasonably a violation of international law is a matter of legal right, possibly even of legal duty if knowledge and a capacity for action exists. Our resisters who properly invoke the authority of Nuremberg stand on firm legal ground, and should not be sent off to jail, but should be exonerated [p. xxi].

24. The acquittal rate in nonviolent resistance cases citing international law is 10 percent and rising, Boyle estimated in 1988 (p. 287). See *The Nuclear Resister* (note 23) for news of such cases. One factor that may increase acquittals during the 1990s is the work of the Fully Informed Jury Association. Founded in 1989, the FIJA (based in Helmville, MT) proposes to require that "the court must inform the jury of its inherent right to judge both the law and the facts," a seemingly absolute power because the U.S. legal system "protects defendants from being tried twice for the same crime" ("ordinarily") and "protects jurors from being punished for their verdicts." FIJA's lobbyists already operate in 35 states. Quoted from "Courtroom Putsch? Jurors Should Reject Laws They Don't Like, Activist Group Argues" (*Wall Street Journal*, January 4, 1991, p. A1).

25. Part of the debate in the Gulf crisis was over whether to "rely on sanctions or authorize the use of force." The terms of this

debate were misleading. Historical experience has already established that nonviolent sanctions are, in fact, a form of force, and a powerful one able at times to coerce an aggressor. See Robert A. Irwin, "Coercion, Force, and Nonviolent Sanctions" (1986; 17 pp.; available for $2.00 postpaid from the author, c/o Sociology Dept., Brandeis University, P.O. Box 9110, Waltham, MA 02254-9110. Concerning civilian-based defense, a policy whereby a society can prepare to defend itself against aggression by use of nonviolent struggle, see *BAPS*, pp. 55-62, 176-177, 269.

26. For an annotated list of recommended periodicals and audio and video news/commentary sources, with suggestions on where to begin, see *BAPS*, pp. 263-278. A national peace organization that can also tell you how to contact other ones is the War Resisters League, 339 Lafayette Ave., New York, NY 10012; (212) 228-0450.

27. See note 3 above.

28. See *BAPS*, pp. 209-214, 249-251, for all you need to know to organize a 7-session or 15-session study group on peace. (Materials are now provided by Pacem in Terris, 1106 Adams St., Wilmington, DE 19801; 302-656-2721.)

29. For nonviolence training, contact the War Resisters League (see note 26) or other national peace organizations they suggest.

30. See *BAPS* (p. 297) or contact WRL for a list of groups. *BAPS* (pp. 151-156) suggests ways being in a group can help one work for peace.

31. Two excellent handbooks are: *Resource Manual for a Living Revolution* (New Society, 1981; 330 pp.; $14.95; order from 1-800-333-9093); and the War Resisters League's *Organizer's Manual* (1981; 222 pp.; see note 26 above to order).

Organizations Working on Middle East Issues

Additional contacts available from the National Campaign for Peace in the Middle East.

American-Arab Affairs Council, 1730 M St NW, Suite 512, Washington, DC 20036　　　　　　Tel: (202) 296-6767

American-Arab Anti-Discrimination Committee, 4201 Connecticut Ave NW, Rm 500, Washington, DC 20008　　　　　　Tel: (202) 244-2990

American Friends Service Committee, Middle East Program, 1501 Cherry St, Philadelphia, PA 19102　　Tel: (215) 241-7000

Americans for Middle East Understanding, 475 Riverside Dr, Rm 771, New York, NY 10115　　　　　　Tel: (212) 870-2053

Arab World and Islamic Resources, 2137 Rose St, Berkeley, CA 94709　　　　　　Tel: (415) 845-6625

Association of Arab-American University Graduates, 556 Trapelo Rd, Belmont, MA 02178　　　　Tel: (617) 484-5483

Campaign for Peace with Justice in the Middle East, c/o American Friends Service Committee, 2161 Massachusetts Ave, Cambridge, MA 02140　　　　　　Tel: (617) 661-6130

Coalition to Stop US Intervention in the Middle East, 36 E 12th St, 6th Floor, New York, NY 10003　　Tel: (212) 254-2295

Fellowship of Reconciliation, Crossing the Line Campaign, PO Box 271, Nyack, NY 10960　　　　　　Tel: (914) 358-4601

Global Exchange: Middle East, 2940 16th St, Rm 307, San Francisco, CA 94103　　　　　　Tel: (415) 255-7296

International Center for Middle East Peace, 15 E 84th St, New York, NY 10028　　　　　　Tel: (212) 599-0917

International Jewish Peace Union, PO Box 20854, Tompkins Sq Sta, New York, NY 10009　　　　　　Tel: (212) 979-8754

Jewish Peace Fellowship, PO Box 278,
Nyack, NY 10960   Tel: (914) 358-4601

Labor Committee on the Middle East, PO Box 421429,
San Francisco, CA 94142

MERIP, see Middle East Research and Information Project

Middle East Children's Alliance, 2140 Shattuck Ave, Rm 207,
Berkeley, CA 94704   Tel: (415) 548-0542

Middle East Institute, 1761 N St NW,
Washington, DC 20036Tel: (202) 785-1141

Middle East Justice Network, PO Box 558,
Cambridge, MA 02238   Tel: (617) 666-8061

Middle East Librarians' Association, Ohio State University,
Main Library, Rm 310, 1858 Neil Ave Mall,
Columbus, OH 43210   Tel: (614) 422-8389

Middle East Research and Information Project,
1500 Massachusetts Ave NW, Rm 119,
Washington, DC 20005   Tel: (202) 223-3677

Middle East Watch, 485 Fifth Ave,
New York, NY 10017   Tel: (212) 840-9460

Middle East Witness, 515 Broadway,
Santa Cruz, CA 95060   Tel: (408) 423-1626

Najda: Women Concerned about the Middle East,
PO Box 7152, Berkeley, CA 94707   Tel: (415) 549-3512

National Association of Arab Americans, 2033 M St NW, 9th
Floor, Washington, DC 20036   Tel: (202) 467-4800

National Campaign for Peace in the Middle East, PO Box
3009, Church St Sta, New York, NY 10033 Tel: (212)727-3069

National Council in US-Arab Relations, 1625 Eye St NW,
Washington, DC 20006   Tel: (202) 293-0801

National Mobilization for Survival, 45 John St, Rm 811,
New York, NY 10038   Tel: (212) 385-2222

Palestine Solidarity Committee, 11 John Street, Suite 806,
New York, NY 10038   Tel: (212) 227-1435

PeaceNet, 3228 Sacramento St, San Francisco,
CA 94115   Tel: (415) 923-0900

Third World Resources, Middle East Task Force, 464 19th St,
Oakland, CA 94612   Tel: (415) 835-4692

Union of Palestine Women's Associations, P.O. Box 533,
Chicago, IL   Tel: (312) 436-6060

US Interreligious Committee for Peace in the Middle East,
Green and Westview, Philadelphia, PA 19119
                                          Tel: (215) 438-4142

War Resisters League, 339 Lafayette St,
New York, NY 10012   Tel: (212) 228-0450

About the Contributors

Eqbal Ahmad is Professor of Politics at Hampshire College in western Massachusetts. A fellow of the Institute for Policy Studies, he has lectured and published widely on Middle East and third world issues. He currently serves as joint editor of the British journal *Race & Class.*

Hady Amr, a graduate of Tufts University, has lived in several Middle Eastern countries. He is the national coordinator of the Middle East Justice Network.

Naseer Aruri is Professor of Political Science at Southeastern Massachusetts University. The author of *Jordan: A Study in Political Development* and *Occupation: Israel over Palestine,* he is a member of the board of directors of Amnesty International U.S.A. and of Middle East Watch, and is a founding member of the Arab Organization of Human Rights.

Greg Bates is the publisher at Common Courage Press.

Cyrus Bina is a visiting scholar at the Center for Middle Eastern Studies at Harvard University. He was director and Professor of Economics at Olivet College in Michigan and is a member of the editorial board of the *Journal of Economic Democracy.* He is the author of *The Economics of the Oil Crisis* (St. Martin's Press, 1985), and is co-editor of *Modern Capitalism and Islamic Ideology in Iran* (St. Martin's Press, forthcoming).

Jeanne Butterfield is the Executive Director of the Palestine Solidarity Committee and chairperson of the North American Coordinating Committee for Nongovernmental Organizations on the Question of Palestine. She has led several fact-finding delegations to the occupied territories and writes regularly on Middle East issues for *The Guardian.*

Noam Chomsky is Institute Professor of Linguistics at the Massachusetts Institute of Technology. He is the author of *Deterring Democracy* (Verso), *Necessary Illusions: Thought Control in Democratic Societies, The Culture of Terrorism, On Power and Ideology: The Managua Lectures,* and *The Fateful Triangle: The United States, Israel, and the Palestinians* (South End Press).

Denis F. Doyon is National Coordinator of the Middle East Peace Education Program of the American Friends Service Committee.

Cynthia Enloe is a professor in the Government and International Relations Department at Clark University in Worcester, Massachusetts.

Rabab Hadi is a Palestinian journalist covering U.N. and U.S. policy in the Middle East for a variety of Palestinian and Arab publications. She writes frequently for *Palestine Focus, The Guardian, Womanews, Washington Report on the Middle East,* and *Christianity and Crisis.* She is a member of the national executive committee of the Palestine Solidarity Committee and the cochair of the Third World Coalition/AFSC.

Robert A. Irwin is a sociologist based at Brandeis University who has lectured and consulted widely on nonviolent struggle and peace strategy. His book *Building a Peace System* (1989; 312 pp.) has been described as "an inspired work" (Elise Boulding) that "may be the most comprehensive manual to date on the interwoven issues of peace, ecology, and social justice" (*The Nonviolent Activist*).

Randy Kehler, a former national coordinator of the Nuclear Weapons Freeze Campaign, is currently co-director of the Working Group on Electoral Democracy.

Erik Larsen is a founding member of GIs for Peace.

Sam Lwin is a 21-year-old student at the New School for Social Research. As of this writing, he awaits court-martial while confined to base at Camp Lejeune.

Manning Marable is Professor of Political Science at the University of Colorado.

Michael Marsh, on the staff of the War Resisters League, does military counseling, outreach to high school and college students, and work with community youth in an attempt to counter the effects of military recruiters. He is active with the New York men's anti-sexist network.

Nancy Murray, who has a Ph.D. in Modern History from Oxford University, is Director of Education at the Civil Liberties Union of Massachusetts. She is also the Director of the Middle East Justice Network based in Cambridge, Massachusetts.

Abbas Nasrawi is Professor of Economics at the University of Vermont, where he has been a faculty member since 1963. In the 1950s, he was on the staff of the Iraqi Ministry of Finance and the Central Bank of Iraq. He has served as a consultant to OPEC and UNESCO. His books include *OPEC in a Changing World Economy,* (1985), *Arab Oil and U.S. Energy Requirements,* (1982).

Sheila Ryan is a writer and researcher on U.S. relations with the Middle East. She has traveled extensively in the Middle East.

Howard Zinn has taught history and political science at Spelman College in Atlanta and at Boston University, where he is now Professor Emeritus. He is the author of *Declarations of Independence: Cross-Examining American Ideology,* and *A People's History of the United States,* among other books.

Stephen Zunes is an assistant professor in the Department of Politics at Whitman College in Walla Walla, Washington. He has written for a variety of academic and general periodicals, and is a contributor to *The Progressive, In These Times,* and the *Christian Science Monitor.* He is the author of two upcoming books: an analysis of U.S. intervention in Latin America and the Middle East during the 1950s, and an overview of the current conflict in the Western Sahara.

About Common Courage Press

Common Courage Press was founded in 1991 to publish books for social justice on race, gender, feminism, economics, ecology, labor, and U.S. domestic and foreign policy. Its mission is to provide analysis of problems from a range of perspectives and aid activists and others, interested in creating fundamental social change in the United States, to develop strategies for action.

You can reach us at:

Common Courage Press
P.O. Box 702
Corner Rte 139 & Jackson Road
Monroe, ME 04951
207-525-0900

Send for a free catalog!